A Language
for the Inward Landscape

A Language
for the Inward Landscape:
spiritual wisdom from the Quaker movement

Brian Drayton
and
William P. Taber, Jr.

TRACT ASSOCIATION OF FRIENDS
PHILADELPHIA, PA

Published 2015 by Tract Association of Friends
Printed in the United States of America

19 18 17 16 15   1 2 3 4

ISBN: 978-1-943290-08-6
Library of Congress Control Number: 2015915143

Dear Hearts, you make your own troubles, by being unwilling and disobedient to that which would lead you. I see there is no way but to go hand in hand with him in all things, running after him without fear or considering, leaving the whole work only to him. If he seem to smile, follow him in fear and love; and if he seem to frown, follow him, and fall into his will, and you shall see he is yours still. *James Nayler*

Therefore come down, come down to the Word of his patience, which is nigh in your hearts, which if you do, he will keep you in the hour of temptation, which shall come to try all upon what foundation they are built; for saith Christ, which is the word of God, *My sheep hear my voice, and they follow me*, and I the Word will get them eternal life, and none can pull them out of his hand, which is that living Word, from whence this testimony of mine proceedeth. *Sarah Jones*

Contents

Welcoming Remarks

To the non-Quaker reader: Welcome!

Even if you are not acquainted with Quakerism, you may find much of interest and value in this book. In order to better understand the experience out of which it arises, you should bear this in mind: Quaker faith and practice are based on the confidence that the spirit of Christ is present to guide the individual and the worshiping group at all times, and that this guidance can be perceived inwardly. For this reason, our traditional worship begins in silence, and without any pre-arrangement, except that someone is designated to bring the meeting to a conclusion. Our experience is that God leads us into the worship that we need. Words of instruction, prayer, exhortation, and testimony arise out of the silence, at the promptings of the Spirit on behalf of the group, and are followed by silence as well. Although this sounds similar to other meditative practices, one important difference is that the worship, both in words and silence, is a shared experience, and we are aware of each other as members of one body.

We make decisions in basically the same way, except that a person chosen by the meeting to preside will take care to bring the business items for community decision, although the agenda arises out of worship, and may move into worship at any time. Decisions are made when unity is sensed by the clerk, the presiding officer, and affirmed by the meeting.

Because of the simplicity and directness of this understanding of worship, any two or more Friends may—with or without pre-arrangement—find themselves in worship during conversation, at work, or in any other setting. Moreover, each of us ideally finds time daily for silent reflection, devotional reading, and prayer. One benefit of this is that any who have such a practice will come to the community worship prepared and ready for the shared encounter with the living God.

Because this experience of immediate encounter is so central to our spirituality, we use the word "meeting" for rather a lot of things: a gathering of one or more persons in worship; a group or congregation that is accustomed to gather at particular times (for example, every Sunday morning); members of a congregation who conduct the community's business once a month ("monthly meeting"); members of several congregations in a region who gather roughly 4 times a year for business ("quarterly meeting"); members of a group of quarterly meetings who gather once a year for business ("yearly meeting") — and this is the highest disciplinary body (apart from some umbrella associations of yearly meetings). So it can be confusing sometimes, but you can usually tell from the context whether an event or an organization is meant.

As you can imagine, more can be said on all these points and more besides. For more introductory information about Quakerism, we encourage you to seek out Friends near you. For help in doing so, you can visit http://www.fwccamericas.org.

To the Quaker reader: Welcome!

Your experience and practice will inform your reading of what follows, and it is our hope that it enriches your spiritual life in turn. It is not intended to prescribe or even advocate for the use of the Quaker language explored in this book, but it may help you get more out of the great storehouse of Quaker spiritual wisdom. It may help you reflect on your own inward experience, and recognize or discover features of that experience that you may not have attended to before. It may also help you think about how to put some of that experience into words, if you are called upon to do so.

With very few exceptions, the voices quoted herein come from the period before separations in the 1800s, when modern Quakerism in its varieties began to take shape. We have found that a sympathetic understanding of the language and the life out of which it sprang can help us speak with Friends of all kinds. This language, and the distinctive understanding of Christianity that it conveys, is a common heritage, shared by Friends on every continent. We hope that, having the Friends quoted herein as company in your own travels across the inward landscape, you may gain in your understanding of the "Gospel as traditionally held by Friends," and grow in your ability to interpret it to others for whom it may be life-giving.

How This Work Came to Be

Sometime in the mid-1980s, Bill Taber, beloved teacher and minister among Friends, conceived of a project he came to call "A language for the inward landscape." One weekend at Pendle Hill, a Quaker retreat center, we were talking about the many passages in the old Quaker journals in which the writers described their inward states, or those of the people and meetings they encountered, using words and phrases that were both puzzling and full of implication. I said, "It almost seems if they are using a technical language." "Oh yes," said Bill, smiling; "I call it a language for the inward landscape."

Bill had a profound interest in, and experience with, the alternative states of consciousness that Friends encounter in their spiritual practice. He found personal renewal in the experience, and a deep kinship with others who traveled inward regardless of their religious affiliation. He also felt that in this experience of the stream of divine life, he was connected with the seekers and finders of times past, especially the Friends who traveled in the ministry, and recounted their travels across the spiritual landscape, which is intricately interwoven with the outward landscape.

Bill also felt it important to help Friends learn more about the language used in these travel accounts, not because the "jargon" itself was precious, but because its complexity and richness reflect a richness and complexity in Quaker spirituality that is too little known among Friends, much less outside the Society. He wanted to make this resource available, as an aid to the spiritual lives of those whose path has led them among Friends.

During the years from the 1980s until his death in 2005, Bill studied and reflected upon this language, and engaged people with it in workshops and presentations. Teaching helped him refine his thinking about the material and the best ways to help people explore it. By the time of his death, he had accumulated several files of notes.

In 2007, about two years after Bill's death, Fran Taber contacted Michael Birkel, of Earlham College, and me to examine and evaluate the files of notes and manuscripts on various subjects that Bill left behind. Our aim was to identify bodies of material that could be prepared for publication. An early fruit of this project was the Pendle Hill Pamphlet, *The mind of Christ: Bill Taber on the meeting for business*, (PHP #406, 2010), edited by Michael Birkel. We agreed that I would work with "the Language" materials for what I came to call the "Taber Papers Project."

The materials on "the Language" consist of perhaps 150 pages of notes, memos, file cards, and outlines. They were organized according to specific workshops where Bill used the notes, and usually include a "thick" outline, in which short phrases or words are occasionally joined by a paragraph of connected prose. Most such manuscripts also include annotations about how Bill wanted to conduct a particular session, or about additional ideas or connections that he wanted to make. There are long lists of words from "the Language," arranged according to various categories, which shifted and morphed over the years, as well as a box of file cards containing illustrative quotations from Quaker writings. The annotations also attest to the way Bill listened carefully during these retreats and workshops, because he notes comments or turns of phrase from participants that he found insightful and helpful at the time. These were incorporated into his growing story. There is also one complete manuscript, "John Woolman's language of the inward landscape," the substance of a presentation he made in Mount Holly, New Jersey, in 1992.

What you have before you is a collaborative document. I built the structure of the book on the outline Bill used for the last workshop he gave on this topic, at the Friends Center in Barnesville, Ohio, a workshop I was able to attend. By the early 2000s, Bill's outlines had stabilized in their general form, and the terms he wanted to bring to Friends' attention also had became a stable, rather long list. Not that his list ever stopped growing: Bill was always glad to come across another term from historical records that deserved to be added to his list. He was also glad to encounter terms from contemporary Friends that seemed to him to be in harmony with the Language of the Inward Landscape as he came to understand it.

Many of his notes, however, remained simply words or phrases in a list. Bill spoke of them freshly each time he presented them, and they were enriched by his description of the feelings or conditions that the terms labeled, and by illustrations from lives — the journals, oral accounts ancient and modern, as well as from his own life and experience. All these terms were interwoven with Bill's understanding of the universal and awesome work of Christ in history, including in our present times, our own lives. The written notes served as anchors and reminders for him—so they are sparse reading indeed.

I have made so bold as to work with this material, in an attempt to make available in printed form one of the major concerns of Bill's later years. I am well acquainted with the journals and other Quaker sources, and have a spirituality that is in sympathy with Bill's. I also benefited from Bill's friendship and mentorship, which were always infused with conversations about the Quaker experience of the Inward Landscape, and its language. I have been very glad for Fran Taber's commentary and guidance, combining her own acute insight about Quaker language and spiritual experience, and her intimate understanding of Bill's thinking on these matters. As I worked with the material, and made choices about how to convey it, my own understandings, sense of organization, as well as my own collections of quotations and writing style have come into play, so that perhaps 75% of the text is by my hand. Alas, in this collaboration I have not been able to consult my co-author.

In trying to convey our understanding of these resources, Bill and I both brought to our Quaker experience the fruits of other sources of nourishment, and it is for this reason that non-Quaker voices are heard occasionally. For example, both Bill and I have been instructed and refreshed by some acquaintance with monastic spirituality; so although Bill's notes contain little or no mention of his readings in this area, I have felt free to bring in such material.

There are places where it has seemed important for one author's voice to come forward explicitly, as when the notes include incidents from his life or personal reflections. I have tried to accomplish this in one of two ways. There may be a sentence that refers to Bill in the third person: "In Bill's classes at Pendle Hill…" In other cases, Bill will be quoted more directly: "Bill sometimes recalled…."

This work is an act of *pietas*, of reverence for a beloved friend and teacher, but I would not have undertaken it if I did not share with Bill the conviction that the resources of classic Quaker practice have much to offer for the nourishment of today's inquiring souls—Quakers and non-Quakers alike.[1]

The aim of any ministry is to encourage others in their walk with God. This book is rooted in our desire to invite or help others to share in the fresh, living experience of Christ's presence and power, which is beyond all language.

—Brian Drayton

---

1 Because this is not intended as a formal study, research studies of Quaker language, sociology, and theology are rarely cited; these and some other items of possible interest, however, appear in occasional footnotes.

I

Introduction

The life of the Spirit cannot fully be captured in words, and Quaker practice is shaped by this truth. Nevertheless, Friends understand and celebrate the central role that language plays in human life. In seeking to describe and cultivate spiritual experience, Quakerism has developed, across its three and one half centuries, a language of inwardness, a "language of the inward landscape." Through this language, Friends have been able to communicate about their inward experiences and their states of consciousness. Even though such language can be interpreted metaphorically, Friends have used it to describe, however imperfectly, realities of consciousness that other Friends could recognize as corresponding to their own experience.

Friends often say that they don't "do" theology very much, that right opinion is less important than right living. It could perhaps better be said that Friends refuse to subordinate spiritual experience, and the transformation of personality, to intellectual formulation, but rather keep them in tension—or active dialogue. Therefore, while Friends rarely undertake systematic theology, there is nevertheless a plentiful Quaker theology of the narrative, pastoral, or prophetic kind (and at some periods, polemical as well). Such writings can at first be puzzling, even off-putting, but they can become a source of nourishment and help, once the language is understood and related to experience, so that the reader can be led through and beyond the words, as if passing through a curtain into a new space. Thus the reader can recognize when she knows something of the experience being described, or find some insight, if she is thirsting for growth in the spiritual life.

Isaac Penington, in his "Short catechism for sake of the simple-hearted," has the learner in his dialogue ask questions about the power that frees from sin and darkness. The inquirer is seeking for doctrine, and hears enough to keep him engaged. But the questioner then seeks to establish the identity of this saving power by name, and gets some surprising answers from A:

Q. *Who is this Saviour?*
A. He is the tree of life I have spoken of all this while, whose leaves have virtue in them to heal the nations. He is the plant of righteousness, the plant of God's right hand. Hast thou ever known such a plant in thee, planted there by the right hand of God? …

Q. *But hath not this Saviour a name? What is his name?*
A. It were better for thee to learn his name by feeling his virtue and power in thy heart, than by rote. Yet, if thou canst receive it, this is his name, *the Light; the Light of the World.* (Penington 1: 123-4)

In the tension that arises in reconciling the lessons from differing sources of revelation, and differing ways to speak of it, Friends never rejected the value of reason, nor the value of much that had been formulated as Christian doctrine. Yet they have always insisted that this cannot ever be separated from the experience of walking with God, confronting God, and being chastised and comforted and taught by the living God. So, like mystics in many traditions, they developed a language for communicating their experience of God, and of other inward experiences, including the conditions of individuals and of meetings. The language at first seems to be founded primarily upon Biblical imagery, but one soon sees that Friends spiritual imagery is richly elaborated upon this foundation. Through much of Quaker history, Friends distrusted many kinds of artistic expression, but they had a poignant appreciation for natural beauty, and for the poetic or evocative effects of this beauty in words.

Quaker spiritual language is alive with sensation —colors, smells, motions, topography. Woolman's *Journal* begins with an image, specifically his vivid childhood memory of a small boy on the way home from school, sitting alone beside the road reading from the 22nd chapter of Revelation, which began, "He showed me a river of water, clear as crystal, proceeding out of the throne of God and the Lamb..." At the age of 36 he could still write of that moment, "the place where I sat and the sweetness that attended my mind remain fresh in my memory" (Woolman 23).

Language and life

One danger of using the term *Inward Landscape* is that it may suggest the spiritual life is only inward and private. Quaker history, and that of most other spiritual traditions, demonstrates that real attention to the inward landscape always leads to outward change in behavior and to patterns of faithfulness that Quakers have called "testimonies." There is a "conversion of manners" that we can all recognize in those who have experienced inward transformation. As Paul writes in Galatians 5:22-23,[2] "the fruit of the Spirit is love, joy, peace, patience, kindness, goodness, faithfulness, gentleness, and self-control." We might add other fruits that seem to accompany the ones on this list, such as persistence and courage, which are important for inward development and outward witness, and the daily conduct of our lives.

Encountering this language today, and living into it, can help us to understand the states of consciousness and stages of spiritual development once common in Quakerism, and in turn probe our own condition. We may not always choose to use this language today—but studying it is useful because this language can help us to be aware of these expanded stages of consciousness and the "spiritual technology" that are a part of our Quaker heritage. An exploration of this language can also lead modern seekers to new ways of inward knowing and discernment, rooted in a seeking and worship "in Spirit and truth," that are not merely an exercise, but an experience of challenge, freedom, and transformation.

Sources and resources

Before turning to the language itself, it may be useful to describe briefly the texts in which these spiritual keywords can be found and seen "in action."

---

2   Translation by author. Unless otherwise noted, biblical quotations throughout this book are from the King James version.

The primary sources are the numerous Quaker journals, or spiritual biographies.[3] These journals began to appear in the late 1600s, and increased in number in succeeding years, with the largest number probably appearing between 1750 and 1850. They continue to be written and sometimes published into the twentieth century. Some journals are collections of letters and tracts, with accompanying material by an editor or editorial committee appointed by a meeting. Others are brief autobiographical sketches that provide testimonies of key events and turning points in the authors' lives (e.g., Mary Penington, Charles Marshall). Yet others are fairly complete narratives and full of detail and incident, the classic example being George Fox's *Journal*, or those of George Whitehead, Catherine Phillips, and John Burnyeat. All are recognizably akin to the Puritan spiritual narratives, such as Bunyan's *Grace Abounding to the Chief of Sinners* (1666), although Quaker journals developed a distinctive style shaped by Quaker theology and community life.[4]

These journals were almost always written by ministers, as a final testimony to the grace of God in their lives, in the hope that the accounts would be encouraging and instructive to their readers. Other sources in this book include meeting epistles, memorial minutes, the diary of John Rutty, and the *Reminiscences* of James Jenkins. The ministers predominate, however, since it is their calling to reflect deeply about inward conditions and states of being, and, as guided by the Light, to put them into words. Many of the journals, after the important descriptions of early life leading to convincement and then growth towards the author's first appearance in the ministry, continue as fairly dry recountings of journeys. Some, however, are far more concerned (or able) to convey something of the journalist's character

---

3   Howard Brinton estimated that perhaps 1000 journals were written, though many exist only in manuscript. See Brinton, *Quaker Journals: varieties of religious experience in the Religious Society of Friends,* Wallingford, PA: Pendle Hill Publications, 1972.

4   For more about the Puritan antecedents, the reader is encouraged to read Bunyan's work, and if curious, to consult two classic studies: Owen C Watkins, *The Puritan experience,* London: Routledge & Kegan Paul, 1972, and Patricia Caldwell, *The Puritan conversion narrative: The beginnings of an American expression,* Cambridge: Cambridge University Press, 1983. For more analysis of the characteristics of the Quaker journals and journalists, see Brinton, *Quaker Journals,* cited above. A penetrating discussion of Quaker language can be found in T. Edmund Harvey, *Quaker Language,* London: Friends Historical Society, 1928.

and conditions in a way that makes them interesting to read—and enables the reader to become acquainted with compelling personalities.[5]

Under their concern for instruction, these journals often describe the writer's 'inward weather,' times of blessing and dryness, and sometimes an acute exploration of events leading up to these times, and factors that helped the author overcome times of weakness and spiritual poverty. This includes the ministers' inward sensing of the condition of the people and meetings they encountered, and how this perception shaped their service in the ministry—in speaking or in keeping still. Journals were written to edify or instruct the generality of Friends, so their language, which may seem obscure to us now, cannot have been seen as esoteric, but as understandable to most Friends. One of the great collections of journals, the *Friends Library*, appeared in serial form in the 1840s, and there are anecdotes of families being called in from the fields to get a taste of the newest installment as it arrived by mail. These journals, along with the Bible and Barclay's *Apology*, were standard reading material in many Quaker homes for decades, and a few journals even now continue to nourish and delight many Friends.

In Bill's classes at Pendle Hill, students reading Quaker texts discovered ordinary English words used in a special way to describe states and qualities of consciousness with the inward work of God. These terms were used and understood by most Friends up through the nineteenth and into twentieth centuries. These terms are always being rediscovered by people reading the old journals, who realize this language helps to illuminate their own experience. So Bill began to build up a list of key words from the "Language for the Inward Landscape." While the language is characteristic of those journals, early Quaker writings are also rich sources, and the Quaker language from all centuries is intricately bound up with Biblical language as well—from histories, prophets, Gospels, psalms, and epistles. Whoever, in seeking God, has expressed pain, discouragement, or gratitude, wonder, joy, or delight in the creation, has contributed to this language.

---

5 For the curious, most of the early journals are of interest: Fox, John Gratton, J. Burnyeat, Stephen Crisp, Thomas Ellwood, George Whitehead, and others. Some favorites from the middle period include Samuel Bownas, Catherine Phillips, Thomas Shillitoe, Edward Hicks, Martha Routh, Job Scott, John Churchman, and of course John Woolman. Wilburite Friends such as Ann Branson and Joseph Edgerton continued the old pattern. More modern in style are those of Louis Taber, Allen Jay, Rufus Jones, James Henderson, and Louise Wilson.

II

Foundational Terms: Wait, Light, Life

Let us begin by exploring some foundational words: *wait*, *light*, and *life*. These terms, some of which are more comfortable for us than others, do not point in different directions. Each of them expresses something of the dynamic reality at the center of Quaker practice.

It is good to stop here and consider the condition out of which Quakerism grew: spiritual hunger, despair, desolation. One can sense the extremity of need recounted by many early Friends, in words like these of George Fox, expressed in his journal:

> I left the separate preachers also, and those called the most experienced people; for I saw there was none among them all that could speak to my condition. And when all my hopes in them and in all men were gone, so that I had nothing outwardly to help me, nor could tell what to do (Fox 11)

The words are so familiar (to Quakers, at least) that we may read them without feeling the anguish and poverty they contain, shared and expressed by many of Fox's contemporaries. The keynote of the time might be summarized by the words of the prophet Amos:

> I will send a famine on the land: not a famine of bread, or a thirst for water, but of hearing the words of the Lord. They shall wander from sea to sea, and from north to east; they shall run to and fro seeking the word of the Lord, but they shall not find it. (Amos 8:11-2)

Our own times seem famished for this word of the Lord, which is not *words*, but reality and power, of the sort that George Fox longed for. Truth seems to hold little value in marketplace or forum; the substance of meaningful work, nourishing community process, and reverent creativity in our occupations, meditations, and recreations seem threatened or emptied by the market mind, the distracted heart, the sated ear. If the world is filled with wonders, and humans can be so breathtakingly compassionate, creative, and ungrasping, why are the notes of fear, dislocation, and hopelessness so loud in our discourse and clear in our faces? We starve for meaning, a deep-rooted joy, and the love that builds up and heals, summarized as the Word or Life or Presence of God: "As the hart panteth after the water brooks, so panteth my soul after thee, O God" (Psalm 42:1).

Early Friends, too, were brought to a place of need that no human agency could satisfy by political, intellectual, or other means. The religious institutions of their time seemed to be as empty of power and truth as any other element of society, and so in the end, these Friends were thrown back to the very root of uncomprehending dependence upon a God whose intentions and actions could seem as removed and disinterested as the God who answered Job, thundering his transcendence. Friends, freed from dependence on false hopes, were led to stand and wait in a time of darkness and disorientation. They found

> no outward ceremony, no words, yea not the best and purest words, even the words of Scripture, able to satisfy their weary and afflicted souls; because where all these may be, the life, power, and virtue which make such things effectual may be wanting. Such, I say, were necessitated to cease from all outwards and to be silent before the Lord. (Barclay 297)

In that desert place, they found themselves visited and liberated by a God of love and judgment, healing and humility, who was both the eternal Word, and the teaching, healing Christ, alive and working in and through them, and seeking the reconciliation of all creation.

Sing and rejoice, you children of the Day and of the Light. For the Lord is at work in this thick night of darkness that may be felt. (Fox, Epistle 227)

As the Reformation continued into the seventeenth century, and social upheavals robbed the established order of credibility, in the eyes of the spiritually alert, seekers in many places in England and Europe began a practice of waiting in silence and abstaining from customary worship. In Germany, the followers of the spiritual reformer Sebastian Franck were led to the practice of "Stillstand," calling a halt with respect to outward spiritual practices that they felt were no longer acceptable in the eyes of the Lord, and awaiting guidance. In a similar movement, and apparently uninfluenced by the continental groups, earnest people across England were "brought off" from their accustomed practices, and led to sit in silence before preaching, teaching, praying, or singing hymns. Friends in Mobberley (Cheshire) recalled Thomas Yarwood,

who sometime after his convincement had his mouth opened to Preach Truth, and was Moved of the Lord to visit a people...whose Custom was when met together neither To preach nor pray vocally butt to Read the Scriptures & Discourse of Religion, Expecting a farther Manifestation. (*First Publishers of Truth* 18)

They saw themselves re-enacting the endurance, and the expectancy, that characterized the Israel into which Jesus was born, and they found deliverance as they

learned to wait upon God in the measure of life and grace received from him...and feel after this inward Seed of Life; that, as it moveth, they may move with it, and acted by its power and influenced, whether to pray, preach or sing. (Barclay 297)

* * *

Waiting, watching

Waiting was thus first a gesture of need, endurance, and wordless faith, but it can be now and always an opportunity to rediscover where our limits, wounds, and hunger lie: "Blessed are those who hunger and thirst for righteousness" (Matthew 5:6). We dare not let our waiting be routine and lifeless. The terms *wait* and *waiting* are in current use among Quakers, and at best, these words still name a living experience.

We must not get too comfortable with these familiar words, but instead rediscover the risk and inward poverty that make them a spiritual imperative. Understood in that light, waiting is the door into the radical restructuring of world-view that Fox, and many Friends since, both experienced and preached. As we wait, we are sometimes able to drop into a consciousness of deeper Life, which we can allow to enter into us.

The term *wait* has encompassed many levels of meaning for Fox and succeeding generations of Friends. It did not mean just allowing the passage of time, although it included that idea —we can recall the incident in which George Fox once waited for three hours before finally speaking to a large group of people. Rather, waiting as a spiritual practice, or spiritual state, might be thought of as a total, though relaxed, focus, or as a way of being completely present, as if "waiting on" a king (or a table in a restaurant), a state of being alertly present, ready to respond to any request or direction. When we recall the famous "wait" text from Isaiah, we get a glimpse of something that includes both the passive/receptive and the active/responsive aspects of waiting: "But they that wait upon the Lord shall renew their strength; they shall mount up with wings as eagles; they shall run and not be weary; and they shall walk and not faint" (Isaiah 40:31).

Such waiting does have an element of passivity, such as when one waits for something to emerge into consciousness. At other times, waiting becomes a deep resting, without agenda. The outcome of such waiting is usually a sense of having been nourished or fed on some deep level. Francis Howgill writes:

> All therefore that see your darkness that you live in, return home, and that which is low mind [that is, "pay heed to that which is low"], the meek Spirit, and be not forward nor rash, but stand still in quietness and meekness, that the still Voice you may hear, which till you come down within, you cannot hear. (Howgill 47)

Yet waiting can also be seen as an action of conscious focus, as an act of will to let go of distractions, fears or impulses that keep us from the true center of knowing and nurture. This focus can also be experienced as an act of love reaching out to love, or as an act of will responding to our profound desire to be totally present to that which is most relevant and most real. Such waiting could also sometimes be described as a relaxing into the arms of divine providence with a deep trust in whatever is to happen, or be, concerning us.

A close relative of *wait* in this active sense is *watch*, a word that connects waiting and seeking to the work of prophecy. Early Friends, as they found in their waiting the insistent call of the Lord to righteousness, and the power to attain to it, joined in the great stream of watchers, looking towards God for answers to their need. They also looked at the condition of themselves and other people with eyes freshly cleansed and keen. The sense of power and mystery they experienced, which we can taste even now, shines through this story from the early days of the Quaker explosion:

> In or about the year 1655 came a servant of the Lord, but a stranger outwardly, called Thomas Parrish...to a meeting of the people called Independents...And after some time he had waited on the Lord in spirit, he had an opportunity to speak, all being silent. He said by way of exhortation, "Keep to the Lord's watch!" These words, being spake in the power of God, had its operation upon all or most of the meeting, so that they felt some great dread or fear upon their spirits...some thought to have spake... but could not because of the unusual awe that was on their spirits. After a little time he spake again, saying, "What I say unto you, I say unto all: Watch!"[6] [in] such a voice that most of the hearers had never heard before, that carried such great authority that they were

---

6   Quoting Mark 13:37, a passage in which Jesus warns his hearers to be ready and alert for God's appearance, "lest coming suddenly he find you sleeping." The time we have is for us the end time. As Fox wrote (Epistle 5), "You have no time but this present time. Therefore prize your time for your souls' sake." See also his epistle 405: " I desire that you may all improve your gifts and talents, and not hide them in a napkin, lest they be taken from you; and not to put your candle under a bushel, lest it go out; and not to be like the foolish virgins...Such were not diligent in the work of God, nor in the concerns of the Lord, nor in their own particulars. And therefore my desires are, that you may all be diligent, serving the Lord and minding his glory, and the prosperity of his truth, this little time that you have left to live."

all necessitated to be subject to the power, though it was a great cross to their wills to sit in silence, though it was but a little time. Then he spake again these words: "Where are your minds now? Wandering abroad? Or in the spirit watching to the Lord?" Then he went on turning their minds to the spirit of Christ by which some of them knew he spake...one in the meeting later said, he blessed God that he had heard the voice of his spirit that day." (*First Publishers of Truth*, 115-116)

It is important to remember what or who we are waiting for (or upon)—and also that we cannot always know what we will find in or through our waiting. After years of seeking and doubt brought him to the recognition that there is one, even Christ Jesus, who could speak to his condition, George Fox received that discovery with joy—but the gift kept unfolding, in ways he could not predict! Listen to this remarkable passage from his journal:

Now I was come up in spirit through the flaming sword, into the paradise of God. All things were new; and all the creation gave unto me another smell than before, beyond what words can utter. I knew nothing but pureness, and innocency, and righteousness; being renewed into the image of God by Christ Jesus, to the state of Adam, which he was in before he fell. The creation was opened to me; and it was showed me how all things had their names given them according to their nature and virtue.

I was at a stand in my mind whether I should practice physic for the good of mankind, seeing the nature and virtues of things were so opened to me by the Lord. But I was immediately taken up in spirit to see into another or more steadfast state than Adam's innocency, even into a state in Christ Jesus that should never fall. And the Lord showed me that such as were faithful to Him, in the power and light of Christ, should come up into that state in which Adam was before he fell; in which the admirable works of the creation, and the virtues thereof, may be known, through the openings of that divine Word of wisdom and power by which they were made.

Great things did the Lord lead me into, and wonderful depths were opened unto me, beyond what can by words be declared; but as people come into subjection to the Spirit of God, and grow up in the image and power of the Almighty, they may receive the Word of wisdom that opens all things, and come to know the hidden unity in the Eternal Being. (27-28)

Fox saw a new landscape opening before him—a landscape so illuminated by the Light by which he was enabled to see, that it was transformed. He recognized in these breakthrough moments that the very personal, inward experience he was having revealed his connectedness to everything and everyone else. He was given a glimpse of how God loves the creation, and has woven it together into a fabric or network, whose essence can be compassion and mutual service, rather than competition and self-serving. These insights are the fruits of his thirst for integrity or righteousness, which set him on his search. In his times of waiting, he knew what he was waiting for, which was the quiet but dynamic, creative power he encountered in these days of great openings.

Our waiting, if it is to be an opening to spiritual growth, should not be seen primarily as a search for relaxation and "recharging," but as an encounter with the living God. The practice of retirement starts simply, with the opening up of space in our schedules. The disciplines related to time are central to many problems we face, as individuals and as members of a spiritual community. Time is one of the most sacred resources we have. As Frances Taber wrote: "Filling the time is in truth the real danger we face as a religious society. It is a problem endemic to our age" (F. Taber 31). We can respond most directly, and most radically, by finding ways to reclaim time and inward attention. In doing so, remember that anything worth doing is worth doing badly (not up to our envisioned standards) —at first. Learning from mistakes is a productive path forward, as any artist or scientist knows —if we keep our eye on our goal, "failure" can be a productive discipline.

I suspect that it is precisely when we are most in need of silent spaces in our lives that it's hardest to work them in. Yet some busy people have told me how they slip times of meditation into cracks in the day or into the early morning before work. The yearning for the deep silent spaces is a strong tug for one who has known —and been known by—the Presence. The logical conclusion of right use of time is no less than a total reordering of one's life with God at the center. Perhaps a good start is to answer the query, "Whose time is it?" (Fardelmann, "Right Use," 9)

Even though, in Quaker practice, this waiting does usually require a significant passage of time—such as an hour or more for a typical meeting for worship, and perhaps half an hour for daily personal retirement—it is important to be aware that such waiting *can* be almost instantaneous. It need only be just long enough "to cross the threshold" to an altered state of consciousness, of being intensely and fully present. Once we have learned the spirit and the stance of waiting, we can sometimes just go to that inward place and quickly get the answer we need, even sometimes in the midst of conversation or other outward activity, as Friends were led to do even many times during a day. When we are waiting whole-heartedly, it is as if the Holy Spirit can expand time.

By practicing waiting, we can learn to dwell in watchfulness, maintaining an inward attention on our condition, not far from the threshold of prayer, and become increasingly sensitive to the little hints and motions of the Spirit. Friends spoke of keeping the "daily watch," and sometimes noted when they did or did not do so. The painfully observant John Rutty, who carried on a constant struggle with himself, wrote: "Eleventh month 2, 1755: Lay too late for this day. O, where is the holy watching!" (Rutty 44). John Woolman also noted how, in the midst of a domestic dispute in which Woolman was asked to mediate, "there arose some heat in the minds of the parties, and one valuable Friend got off his watch," expressing himself in a way that the younger Woolman felt required to remonstrate against, in private (Woolman 35).

* * *

In his journal, John Woolman provides many examples of his skill in waiting, which can be instructive to reflect upon; we will mention only one. During his 1757 ministry among Friends in North Carolina, he attended monthly meeting at Simons Creek, where my mind was exercised concerning the poor slaves, but did not feel clear to speak. And in this condition I was bowed in spirit before the Lord, and with tears and supplications besought him to so open my understanding that I might know his will concerning me, and at length my mind was settled in silence. (70)

Then near the end of the meeting, one of the local members arose with a concern about slaves, with which many others then united.

Although Woolman did not say so, this incident illustrated his absolute trust in, and practice with, the process of waiting. He had known that he must not speak even this burning concern unless he felt inwardly clear to do so, and thus he allowed his mind to be, as he put it, "settled in silence." The silence made it possible for a local Friend to raise the concern, so that the concern arose from the grassroots, rather than from a visiting stranger.

There is waiting of another kind, when we are in the middle of some important spiritual process, awaiting we know not what. Some Christian mystics have described the "dark night of the soul,"[7] when a sense of spiritual poverty is joined to a feeling that God has somehow for the time withdrawn. Classic Quaker ministers frequently report such "dark night journeys," as Sandra Cronk called them.[8] For example, they often report painful barren periods, in which for meeting after meeting the ministers are "shut up," that is, they feel empty of words and commanded to wait in patient silence, no matter how much inward work they are undergoing, and however uncomfortable they feel. Such times are different from meetings when it feels that there is a positive duty to "be an example of silence" to the body, or when, as these ministers sometimes wrote, a blessed meeting passed with no sense of requirement to speak, but permission to rest and take spiritual nourishment for themselves.

These times of enforced waiting, when the silence itself is the command we receive, can be painful. It is puzzling if the minister has followed a calling, as carefully and fully as she could—for example, traveling with a minute from meeting, perhaps appointing meetings for worship—and

---

7   See John of the Cross, *Dark Night of the Soul*. Tr. M. Starr. New York: Riverhead Books, 2002.

8   See Sandra Cronk, *Dark Night Journey: Inward re-patterning toward a life centered in God*. Wallingford, PA: Pendle Hill Publications, 1991.

then has nothing to offer. There can be a sense of oppression, or sometimes even depression; the phrase "stripped" is often used, meaning that all one's usual sense of self-confidence and competence have been stripped away. At such times the minister has to work hard not to act solely in order to meet his/her own expectations, or those of the Friends who came to hear a visiting prophet. Sometimes the minister (or any of us) must do some inward work, before *emptiness* becomes *waiting*.

One essential ingredient in this waiting that comes with experience is the confidence that the stream of divine life is always flowing, and the patient seeker, even in a time of darkness, will certainly find his or her way to it again. Martha Braithwaite, a British minister of the nineteenth century, found herself often tried by weakness and dejection while traveling in her youth, after exhilarating times when she felt she was "well used" in ministry. She brought this sense of bereavement into her prayer, and was led to see how the emptiness was actually a time to wait and receive, perhaps in ways she could not identify.

> I soon found my mind dipped into fresh baptisms as we rode along. Oh, these ' deaths oft,' how the creaturely part does shrink from passing through them, and yet they are I believe indispensably necessary, nor is it any wonder if vessels in use need more washing and cleansing than those which may be laid up on the shelf. (Emmott 55-6)

Braithwaite thus saw that the swings of mood were in fact part of a larger whole, which was her being consistently ready—prepared and prepared again—during a time of intensive service. As Sandra Cronk tells us, one can come to see that this experience can be a door to an increasing integration of one's will and personality with God's will and life, a "repatterning."

Not always do we know why we endure such times, and perhaps there is no purpose. We are wise not to overthink, but to keep to the simplicity of waiting. As James Nayler wrote:

> Art thou in the Darkness? Mind it not, for if thou dost it will fill thee more, but stand still and act not, and wait in patience till Light arises out of Darkness to lead thee. Art thou wounded in

conscience? Feed not there, but abide in the Light which leads to Grace and Truth, which teaches to deny, and puts off the weight, and removes the cause, and brings saving health to Light. (4: 235)

* * *

Light

The word "light" is much beloved of Friends nowadays, as it was among the early Friends. While it remains a central Quaker term, however, it has acquired modern meanings or overtones that differ in important respects from its traditional understanding. In Quaker language, it is a metaphor that is more, much more, than a metaphor!

In approaching the Quaker understanding of the Light, we often look to the passage in John's Gospel, which, Barclay tells us, was sometimes termed the "Quaker scripture" by opponents in the seventeenth century:

In the beginning was the Word, and the Word was with God, and the Word was God. The same was in the beginning with God. All things were made by him; and without him was not any thing made that was made. In him was life; and the life was the light of men. And the light shineth in darkness; and the darkness comprehended it not. ...

That was the true Light, which lighteth every man that cometh into the world. He was in the world, and the world was made by him, and the world knew him not. (John 1:1-10)[9]

It must be emphasized, however, that the first Friends did not start with this and other "Light" passages in the Bible, and then set out to make them part of living experience. Nor was it that these seekers read the Scriptures, and found the language to answer their questions, ending their search. The "light and life" passages had power for Friends because

---

9   The Spirit-filled and mystical gospel of John was congenial to Friends on many additional counts. A good place to explore this is Howard Brinton's *The Religious Philosophy of Quakerism*. Wallingford, PA: Pendle Hill Publications, 1973.

they expressed the way in which these spiritual pilgrims encountered Christ among them. The passage from Isaac Penington noted above continues:

> Q. *But hath not this Saviour a name? What is his name?*
> A. It were better for thee to learn his name by feeling his virtue and power in thy heart, than by rote. Yet, if thou canst receive it, this is his name, *the Light; the Light of the World;* a light to enlighten the Gentiles, that he may convert and make them God's Israel, and become their glory. ...we call him light, because the Father of lights hath peculiarly chosen this name for him, to make him known to his people in this age by, and hath thus made him manifest to us. And by thus receiving him under this name, we come to know his other names. (1: 123)

When one reads writings from the early days of the movement, it seems clear that there were several characteristic experiences of light. Indeed, the many operations of the Light of Christ which Friends testified to can be seen already in the gospel of John, and their intimate knowledge of the gospel would have enriched and informed their experience of this light. The Word (*logos*) is God creative; in the Word is life, which is light to every one; its mere presence divides true from false, light from dark, the tender heart from the hardened one. Jesus embodies this light and word, and in him, whose final and cardinal commandment is love, can be found the path, the truth we seek for our reconciliation with God, and abundant life, and we are in every case to return to the Light, the Word, for guidance, safety, healing, renewal.[10]

The operations of the light we wish to hold up here are:

Light as illumination. The first is the basic human experience of walking in the night, unable to see things rightly, or knowing how to proceed. Night

---

10 In this understanding of Christ as active Word and healing Light, Friends are near in spirit to many throughout history. For example, Erasmus says in *Ciceronianus* that the sick soul can rely on "Doctor Logos" at need.

is a time of disorientation and sometimes fear, when our most important sense, sight, is limited so that the visible world contracts around us, loses color and many dimensions of meaning. It is easy to become disoriented, and to walk in the wrong direction, even into danger. If we have watched long through the night, how grateful we are to see the first light of dawn, or the glimmer of a friend's lantern! "The people that walked in darkness, have seen a great light, and they that walked in the shadow of death, upon them hath a light shined!" (Isaiah 9:2).

The experience of being able to see and to be oriented is expressed in Paul's great exhortation, in Ephesians 5:8: "ye were sometimes darkness, but now are ye light in the Lord; walk as children of light." And so Friends called themselves Children of the Light, the children of the Father of Lights (James 1:17).

We are able to act freely in the daylight, and it is during the day that we can enjoy what Merton calls "the great luminous smiles of business and production." As Jesus said, "I must work the works of him that sent me, while it is day: the night cometh, when no man can work" (John 9:4).

This sense of Light as illumination, as clarified understanding or gentle guidance, shows up, too, in some Friends' reliance on it in discernment. When confronted with a choice or dilemma, a Friend might center down and wait to see which path seems to be bathed in more light. If no other guidance is forthcoming, the Light's presence itself may indicate where it is safe to go. Penington, that shrewd observer of spiritual dynamics, says that this living Light both makes the path visible, and gives us the ability to step upon it:

There is a creating, a quickening power in the light, which begets a little life, and that can answer the voice of the living power. (1: 125)

Light as truth-revealer. But the illumination of the Inward Landscape can be terrifying too, because it reveals and challenges us by what it shows us about our selfishness, pride, violent thoughts, or separation from God. This experience of the Light is also described in John's Gospel: "And the light shineth in the darkness; and the darkness comprehended it not" (1:5).

And later: "For God did not send the Son into the world to judge the world, but so that the world might be saved through him...but whoever does not believe is judged...for this is the judgment, that the light came into the world, and people cherished the darkness rather than the light" (John 3:17-19).[11] As George Fox said, the light shows us what and who we are, as well as where help can come from:

> Dwelling in this light, it will discover to thee the body of sin, and thy corruptions and fallen estate, where thou art, and multitude of thoughts. (*Works* iv: 17)

Fox himself discovered in his seeking time how he had within him the potential for sin, even though he had, as he says in his journal, known purity and righteousness from an early age. Yet as the Lord worked in him, he was shown the ocean of darkness and death, and also

> the Lord showed me that the natures of those things, which were hurtful without, were within, in the hearts and minds of wicked men. The natures of dogs, swine, vipers, of Sodom and Egypt, Pharaoh, Cain, Ishmael, Esau, etc.; the natures of these I saw within, though people had been looking without. I cried to the Lord, saying, "Why should I be thus, seeing I was never addicted to commit those evils?" (Fox, *Journal* 19)

When we come into the Presence, and inward stillness, we may well find ourselves afflicted by the realization of the great distance between our current selves and the God whose beautiful holiness we seek, whose company we wish to keep. This is a feeling as old as Adam and Eve, who, armed with the knowledge of good and evil, felt compelled to hide from the Creator as he walked, seeking their company in the cool of the day.

Earlier Friends used language of sin, depravity, and condemnation in describing their dejection as they stood in the Light and saw their darkness. For many modern Friends, the idea of human depravity, which Friends felt

---

11 Translated by author.

keenly in former centuries, may not ring true. We may feel that, as part of a comfortable and polite society, and wrapped in conventional morality, we have been spared from sinning greatly, as far as we know.

But standing in the Light, we can find deeply embedded convictions that keep us far off from God, even as we utter the Divine's names with longing. Many of us suspect that we are unworthy of others' consideration, of love or even respect, and even more so of God's. We may be inhibited by fear of what may come to us if we open too much. Hence we are religious without the warm dangers of enthusiasm, which have been devalued since the Age of Reason.[12] We are likely to avoid whole-heartedness as a defensive maneuver against the deeps and wildernesses that may come if we fall into the hands of the living God, and against what this whole-heartedness may uncover in ourselves. As the Catholic author Thomas Merton wrote:

> Perhaps I am stronger than I think. Perhaps I am even afraid of my strength, and turn it against myself, thus making myself weak. Making myself secure. Making myself guilty. Perhaps I am most afraid of the strength of God in me. Perhaps I would rather be guilty and weak in myself, than strong in him whom I cannot understand. (Merton 146)

We may also find that we are committed to, or habituated to, patterns of thought and behavior that do in fact carry us out of the Light, and make us reluctant to come too far into it. "Who can understand his errors? Keep back thy servant from secret faults," says Psalm 19:12, but how much of our self-deprecating humor shows that we know very well where there are aspects of our life and conduct that are inconsistent with the self that would emerge under God's guidance, clarity, and power? And we are inclined to stay as we are, in an uneasy truce that is not peace. No wonder generations of Friends ministers, when their sight was clear, felt called (feel called) to cry with the prophet Amos, "Woe to you that dwell at ease in Zion!" (6:1).

---

12 "Religious without enthusiasm" was a well-known compliment in the 18th century. See P.H. Osmund, *The Mystical Poets of the English Church* (London: Society for Promoting Christian Knowledge, 1919), 262, for example.

But we should bear in mind that the Quaker spiritual journey always involves increasing self-awareness, and greater acuteness of observation of our own and others' condition. We are not on that path if our spiritual work results in greater and greater self-absorption. Woolman writes:

> The natural mind is active about the things of this life, and in this natural activity business is proposed and a will is formed in us to go forward in it. And so long as this natural will remains unsubjected, so long there remains an obstruction to the clearness of Divine light operating in us; but when we love God with all our heart and with all our strength, in this love we love our neighbor as ourselves; and a tenderness of heart is felt towards all people for whom Christ died, even those who, as to outward circumstances, may be to us as the Jews were to the Samaritans. "Who is my neighbor?" See this question answered by our Saviour, Luke x. 30. In this love we can say that Jesus is the Lord ... (177)

"Where is the poison, there is the antidote!" The Light can be comforting, giving energy just as we feel warmth from the sun, and Light can show a way, and offer healing in the midst of darkness, or through it. Thus, when George Fox was most struck in his early seeking days by the extent and power of Darkness, he was immediately reassured, not that that this ocean of death was unreal, or to be discounted, but that there was also an ocean of light and life, which flowed over the night of death. This vision must have come powerfully back to him sometimes, when he could assert in times of adversity, "the power of the Lord is over all."

> Whatsoever you see yourselves addicted to, temptation, corruption, uncleanness, etc., then you think you shall never overcome. Earthly reason will tell you what you shall lose. Hearken not to that, but stand still in the Light that shows them to you, and then strength comes from the Lord, and help, contrary to your expectation. Then you grow up in peace, and no trouble shall move you. (Fox, Epistle 10)

Penington writes about how exposure by the Light of our encumbered natures comes even as we feel the mildest, humblest movements towards —what destination? For some it may be "rest," or "freedom," "newness of life," or "peace": What is your word for it?

> Hast thou never found a true, honest breathing towards God? Hast thou never found sin not an imaginary, but a real burden? This was from life: there was somewhat begotten of God in thee, which felt this. It was not the flesh and blood in thee; but somewhat from above... In the light which shines in all, and visits all, there is the power; and this power strives with the creature to work itself into the creature; and where there hath been the least breathing after life, there hath been a taste of the power: for this came from it. But the great deceiver of souls lifts up men's minds in the imagination to look for some great appearance of power, and so they slight and overlook the day of small things, and neglect receiving the beginning of that, which in the issue would be the thing they look for. Waiting in that which is low and little in the heart, the power enters, the seed grows, the kingdom is felt and daily more and more revealed in the power. And this is the true door and way to the thing: take heed of climbing over it. (Penington 1: 125)

This Light can be invisible until there is something to illuminate, and it can be blinding if we look at its source. It is at once revealer, judge, and healer. As Penn wrote:

> Wherefore, O friends, turn in, turn in, I beseech you! Where is the poison, there is the antidote; there you want [are in need of] Christ, and there you must find him; and blessed be God, there you may find him. Seek and you shall find, I testify for God. (Penn 83)

Light as the source of unity. The Light in its healing and revealing power enables us, and guides us into a unity in the divine life that is constantly being renewed. Where the Light is at work, the barriers of ego, culture, and the demands and anxieties of our lifestyles and personalities are dissolved and overcome.

> In the Light wait and walk, that you may have fellowship one with another...All who in the Light do dwell, which comes from Christ, come to receive the eternal Life. Here the Love of God is shed abroad in the heart. Dwelling in Love, you dwell in God and from the Life the eternal Love does flow, which Life comes from the Father of Life, whose love does not change. And so with the Light ... you will come to witness the Faith unfeigned, the humility unfeigned and the faith which works by love, which purifies the heart. (Fox, Epistle 149)

Modern Quaker uses of "light." We have been considering some of the classic teaching about the Light, but though Friends still use this metaphor today, it sometimes has nuances that differ from those of the past.

Sometimes the word *light* serves as a way to speak of the Divine in a tone that feels intimate, in the way that seeing is intimate: a very personal interaction with a Reality, which does not require us to put names on the experience, nor give an account in words:

> The Light Within, which is the central Quaker idea, is no abstract phrase. It is an experience. It is a type of religion that turns away from arid theological notions and that insists instead upon a real and vital experience of God revealed to persons in their own souls, in their own personal lives.... We no more need to go somewhere to find God than the fish needs to soar to find the ocean or the eagle needs to plunge to find the air.... The pioneer Quakers believed with all their minds and strength that something like that was true, that they had discovered it, tested it, and were themselves a demonstration of it. (Jones, *An Interpretation of Quakerism*).

The language of the Light also allows Friends to speak on the basis of their experience, while avoiding words that may seem theologically challenging in our very diverse communities. Metaphors using *light* are common in English, and many of the most commonplace phrases (or even clichés) capture some of the nuances of the traditional Quaker Light language: "a light at the end of the tunnel," "a light came on and I realized..." Indeed, the *light* language is so rooted in primal experience that it is naturally to be found in every religious tradition. Thus, the essential root of the Quaker language in the identification of Christ as the Light, along with the other New Testament *light* language, can easily fade out of consciousness, with no apparent loss.

In areas of Quakerdom in which the language about "the Light within" has thus come to be used in the context of a great deal of theological diversity or uncertainty, it is important to ask: What do we mean when we say, "I will hold you in the Light"? When the Light is identified, as traditionally, with the inward presence and work of Christ, this identification implies some expectations about spiritual experience. The Light is interpreted by what we learn of Christ in the Gospels and New Testament letters; at the same time, the scriptural record is also interpreted by our encounter with the living Christ in ourselves and others. If the Light is not linked with the spirit of Christ, then we must seek other ways to understand what in our experience is in harmony with the Light that we know, and what is not. So it is good to take some time in our meetings to ask each other with real interest such concrete questions as:

- What do you mean by the Light, and is that an important way you experience God's presence and action? How does your experience relate to that of Penington, quoted above?

- Have you experienced the Light visually? Do you know someone who has or usually does?

- What are the ways you distinguish between some prompting or teaching of the Light, and a prompting or urging from some other source?

- What is the relation between the Light you experience and that which I experience?

Rufus Jones argued strongly that Quakerism is a distinctive manifestation of mystical religion that is kindred with other such manifestations throughout Christian history, and indeed within other religious traditions as well. In the decades since his time, there has been vigorous debate about his interpretation of early Quakerism's relationship with other mystical movements. However the history developed, the experience of the Light as described by many Friends in every generation seems to exemplify what R.M. Bucke called "cosmic consciousness," which is a radical change of perspective and priorities about one's self and one's actions, and about the being and actions of others.[13] Such a shift of consciousness can be brought about by many events and experiences; but living in the Light, Friends have discovered, is a way to absorb and respond with growing integrity to a vision that combines compassion and judgment, love, and the necessity for a growth in freedom to embody that love. Sometimes early Friends spoke of the message that emerged from this consciousness as *Truth*, to which we will return in the next chapter.

* * *

Life

Life is so central to Friends' experience that it appears throughout this book. Although we can say that life refers to a basic characteristic of the living God, it has many shades of meaning in Quaker parlance. Once again, it is good to start with the Gospel of John, and to reflect on some of the biblical resonances of *life* and *living*.

> In the beginning was the word, and the word was with God, and the word was God. The same was in the beginning with God. All things were made by him; and without him was not made anything that was made. In him was life, and the life was the light of men. And the light shineth in darkness, and the darkness comprehended it not. (John 1:1-5)

The word was present in the beginning, and is active now in a myriad of forms and ways; it is life-bringing and creative, and it is as life that the word meets us.[14] Through this word, this loving divine activity, both cosmic and

---

13 See R.M. Bucke, *Cosmic consciousness: A study in the evolution of the human mind*. 1901. Reprint, New York: Cosimo, Inc., 2006.

14 Moreover, it is the divine life that enlightens—the Light is not a human faculty, but an action of the Word.

intimate, the world is brought into being, and sustained. Indeed, the *logos* that is translated as *word* is closely akin to Wisdom, or Sophia, who in Proverbs 8 is portrayed as God's companion in the delight of creation, originating and maintaining all things, healing, enlightening, and inviting all to participate in the divine purpose.

> So, none can see the life but with the light, which from the life comes, which to the life leads all that come. So this that was in the beginning is given to keep in order all the creation. (Nayler 3: 54)

Life is the power of God that flows through Christ the Vine to all its branches, or God's people, who are united into one organic being. This understanding lay behind Fox's outcry concerning the "blood of Christ," which provides a different way to understand this loaded term in Christian language. In 1648, Fox was at Mansfield in Nottinghamshire, among a "great meeting of professors." They were talking about the saving power of blood of Christ shed upon the Cross. Fox felt how this traditional teaching overlooked the present work of Christ, healing and reconciling souls to God, and burst out:

> and as they were discoursing of it, I saw, through the immediate opening of the invisible Spirit, the blood of Christ. And I cried out among them, and said, 'Do ye not see the blood of Christ? see it in your hearts, to sprinkle your hearts and consciences from dead works to serve the living God?' [He comments] 'This startled the professors, who would have the blood only without them and not in them.' (Fox, *Journal* 23).

Fox draws on the image of the Israelite priests' sprinkling the people with the blood (life) of sacrifice, signaling the unity in covenant of God with his people to conjoin vividly the ideas of baptism, communion, life, blood, and the work of salvation as it is accomplished in each of us. Earlier, Fox had been led to see that "what people trampled under foot must be his food," and

> [God] opened it to me how that people and professors did trample upon the life, even the life of Christ was trampled upon; and they

fed upon words, and fed one another with words, but trampled upon the life, and trampled underfoot the blood of the Son of God, which blood was my life. (19)

Thus, *life* is the guiding, clarifying, and uniting action of Christ's spirit, which binds together all who heed God's call.

But *life* also is used to denote inward motions, or outward actions, which feel (to ourselves and others) to have their origin in the divine life, and to help others to turn towards it, or welcome it afresh. So, a concern may be spoken of as "having life in it," and words spoken in ministry may have savor of the life as well. Bill Taber remembered a time early in his ministry when an elder, known for her caution in speech, told him that words he had said in a recent meeting "had life in them." This quiet commendation expressed eloquently the elder's affirmation that the young minister was speaking faithfully. More than that, the comment reflects Friends' conviction and experience that if one is centered in the life, one can recognize its presence in a meeting or an individual. "To keep to the Life" is another way of saying "to keep in step with your Guide." William Penn says:

Oh! feel life in your ministry—let life be your commission, your well-spring and treasury on all such occasions; else you well know, there can be no begetting to God, since nothing can quicken or make people alive to God, but the life of God; and it must be a ministry in and from life, that enlivens any people to God. (67-8)

This *life*, however, is not only a *knowing about*, but an *incorporation* into our own living, actions, and attitudes of what we grasp of the revelation of Christ as God's will. It is expressed, if one may say so, in the language of personality. The re-creation of ourselves is the work done in the light, and to be truthful it must come to be concrete, visceral, and "second nature." Nayler writes powerfully of this process in which one's life and the divine life can be brought into fuller and fuller unity; in his tract *What the Possession of the Living Faith is*, we find together many of the themes—and terms—with which this whole book is concerned:

I have found a measure of the Life of Christ made manifest in my mortal body, in which life alone is the true and eternal union and atonement with the Holy God ... which leads to the beginning of the work of a new creature at this day, and a new birth spiritually begotten, and born and brought to light, without which none can see the kingdom of God, nor enter therein. And this faith does not work by the comprehensions of brain knowledge ... [but] works powerfully in Spirit by love thereto, the mystery whereof is held forth in a pure conscience, working out the old leaven, purifying the Heart, and making all things new, judging, and killing, and crucifying with Christ in Spirit the works of the flesh, and casting out everything in me that is not of God, and renewing in me the things of God in their order, by His mighty working in me, in which the soul is raised out of the grave, and the dead restored to life, actually and not in conceit....

So feeling thy measure of the begettings of God, in it be obedient, and seek not to be above it in anything... Therefore as thou feels faith, love, meekness, gentleness, patience, or any godliness move in the Spirit, therein become obedient with all diligence, and thereby shalt thou know the power thereof against all the contrary motions in thy flesh, so shalt thou learn the salvation of grace unto life eternal, which thou canst never attain by talking or any other way but in the obedience thereof, so shalt thou not receive the grace of God in vain, nor words without the working power of life, whereby the living knowledge of the mystery of godliness will daily increase. (Nayler 4: 70-134 passim)

III

Seed, Sanctification, Measure, Truth

What material is more challenging to work with than human personality? From the time we emerge from our mother's womb, we take on our characters under the influence of family, culture, and experiences, but we also bring our own unique stamp—inclinations, skills, gifts, sensitivities. All these fluid, malleable ingredients of heritage and environment mingle, influencing our individual "material," and take on a shape that seems highly resistant to change, especially as we grow towards adulthood. Yet under the influence of wonder, awe, curiosity, inward poverty, a longing for integrity, a need for healing or consolation, and the life and power of the spirit of Christ, changes can be worked, and creation can be renewed within the framework of our lives. All the "inward landscape" words that we encounter from here onward have to do with this amazing, sometimes frightening process.

* * *

The Seed

When one stills the clamor of inner voices and outer involvements, and comes to a quiet, open condition, one can sense a focus, or a clarity of attention, in which fear and striving do not seem relevant. Time also is not felt, and there is a dawning or fresh sense of possibility, change, and growth. Friends have loved to call this low, beautiful thing of potential and power the *Seed*. The image of a little seed, lying quiet, but stirring against its hard coat to reach into opportunity, can arouse in us the desire to nurture new growth, cultivate the ground, and remove the over-burden that prevents growth towards the Light that is the source of life. Penington writes of his own discovery of clarity after long seeking, study, and struggle:

> ... some may desire to know what I have at last met with? I answer, I have met with the Seed. Understand that word, and thou wilt be satisfied, and inquire no further. I have met with my God; I have met with my Savior; and he hath not been present with me without his salvation ... I have met with the Seed's Father, and in the Seed I have felt him my Father. There I have read his nature, his love, his compassions, his tenderness, which have melted, overcome, and changed my heart before him. (1: 10)

Friends knew this *seed* to be the redeeming presence and promise of God, and to be identical with the risen and active Christ. The *Seed*, Christ, said Fox, is in and over all, and it will grow and triumph over evil in us and in the world, if we recognize the *seed* and cultivate it. We can practice keeping our eye on the precious springing of this life, feeling for its cool and refreshing presence, and staying aware of it. We have been promised that Christ is our elder brother, the first-born of many brethren (Romans 8:29). We are invited to accept his company, to offer hospitality to his life and power, and to participate in the work of healing and creation that is the work of the Word. Penington also writes:

> Give over thine own willing; give over thine own running; give over thine own desiring to know or to be any thing, and sink down to the seed which God sows in the heart, and let that grow in thee, and be in thee, and breathe in thee, and act in thee, and thou shalt find by sweet experience that the Lord knows that, and loves and owns that, and will lead it to the inheritance of life, which is his portion. (2: 205)

Penington's advice is not as simple as the cliché "letting go and letting God," a passive state in which you or I are free to be molded. Even though God makes the first move in stirring up our receptivity or hunger for the divine presence, it is in our living and walking — behaving and intending—in harmony with the guidance of this divine life that we accept and make real our selves as transformed by that light. As Penington continues:

> ...as thou takest up the cross to thyself, and sufferest that to over-spread and become a yoke over thee, thou shalt become renewed, and enjoy life, and the everlasting inheritance in that. (2: 205)

As we live with this Seed and mind the Light, we come to touch, and are enabled to accept, our child-hood of God. We also accept our kinship with Christ, who as Seed and Light, is at work in us, before we even know how to name the power that is searching and soothing us.

> Stand fast, take heed of words without life, spoken from the com-prehensions, for that feeds not the pure seed, but feeds the wisdom which is below, and the itching ears, and so the pure is covered with earth, and the fowls of the air are fed, and no fruit is brought forth to perfection. And take heed of that nature that would know more than God is willing to reveal: for you shall find that unwill-ing to obey what it knows: and take heed of that which desires to appear before men to be commended, for that seldom deserves praise of God. (Nayler, "To All Dear Brethren and Friends in Holderness and the East Parts of Yorkshire," in Whitehead 75)

This *seed* is small and apparently weak, and therefore it is important to be watchful of its growth, and attentive in response. Friends knew that from small beginnings other tendencies and powers could grow in strength that might lead to alienation from God, and spiritual coldness or callousness.

> there is also another seed, which is opposed to that divine seed, which also ramifies as a source of motivation, as a mode of think-ing, as the ground of judgment. It is likely to grow unless opposed, because it is in harmony with, is fed by, the impulses of our bodies, the institutionalized wrongs in our cultures, the delusive security of mental constructs.

Where the life rooted in one seed predominates, the other life is repressed and in time will be eliminated. While we are yet uncommitted and subject to the influence of both, we can feel the two kinds of life at work within and see their fruits in our behavior—now sometimes righteous, now sometimes unrighteous. At first, both impulses are indeed like seeds, tiny and potential, their first stages of growth subtle and hard to detect. We are likely to discount their importance and overlook the power that they can come to have. So little a source of evil cannot be taken seriously, and so it can gain strength while we indulge it; so little a source of good, the seed of God, is not taken seriously, because it seems weak, quiet, and vulnerable, and to cultivate it we must bend low, listen sharply, wait faithfully, and cherish every fruit it bears. (Drayton, *James Nayler* 13)

The Royal Seed

But *seed* can also refer to "descendants," or to "a people sharing common parentage." Fox and some others had in mind that "seed of the woman," the "royal seed," that will struggle with, and overcome, the "seed of the Serpent" (Genesis 3:15). These descendants are gathered by God's work into a shared relationship with the Father, brothers and sisters in the Spirit, and thereby sharing a common life:

To all the Seed of Abraham ... who are of the offspring of David, and of the Church of the first-born; who are the first fruit unto God; ye royal offspring of the Rock of Ages, who have come out of the everlasting washing, my dear brethren, called Quakers, who have eaten your bread with fear and trembling, whom your brethren have cast out; Oh how I love you; my soul is knit unto you; my heart and life breathes after you; I am one with you in suffering and in joy. (Howgill, *The Dawnings* 28)[15]

---

15 The title page of Howgill's works includes this quotation: "And the dragon was wroth with the woman, and went to make war with the remnant of her Seed, which keep the commandments of God, and have the testimony of Jesus Christ" (Rev. 12:17).

Writing from prison and during a time of intense persecution, William Dewsbury declares the stubborn endurance of this "royal seed," and calls upon his brothers and sisters to remember the sweetness of God's working, and the fellowship of all those who are of the royal seed:

> Oh, thou Child of the morning of the pure eternal day of the God of Israel, hearken no longer to the Enemy, who said, there hath none traveled where thou art [traveling,] neither drunk of the cup that thou art drinking; he is a Lyer, who goes about to destroy thy precious soul. In the Word of the Lord God, I declare unto thee, I drank the same Cup, with my faithful Friends, who are born of the royal Seed, every one in their measure have travelled in the same path, and have endured the same temptations, and walked in the Light of the same sparks, and layn down in Sorrow, in the sense of the same misery as thou mourns under this day. No longer lend an ear unto the Enemy, and to the thoughts of thy Heart. Arise, arise, in the Light of the Covenant, and stay thy Heart; and the Lord God he will throw down the enemy of your peace. (Dewsbury 192)

By extension, *seed* can refer to a group of souls gathered, or ready to be gathered. Ministers sometimes felt or saw this seed to be visited with encouragement, and in their writings about it, more than one meaning of *seed* can be heard:

> I was favored with a secret evidence, that the Lord had a seed on that isle, which he designed to visit, and bring to the knowledge of himself, I was therefore thankful that resignation was wrought in me, to obey his will in going there[.] (Routh 202)

> Attended the Select Meeting, wherein was felt close exercise; some of us being dipped into suffering with the suffering seed. (Ratcliff 85)

The phrase "the suffering seed" is telling. A person who is enabled to perceive the spiritual condition of a person or a community may experience that insight as sympathy with the seed, as well as participation in its

43

oppressed condition. Indeed, so poignant is the image that it can be used in instruction, rousing our compassion for the souls whose inward freedom as children of the Light may be constricted by our own behavior:

> when men and women in a discoursitive spirit take upon them to declare the Truth, when the Lord neither calls them, nor speaketh by them; so are the children born of the Royal Seed burthened ... (Dewsbury 320)

As with many terms in this language, there are instances in which different meanings of "seed" may be heard resonating at the same time:

> ... all wait patiently, in the power of the Lord wait...that in the seed ye may be kept which is heir of the power.... For that is it which will keep you out of the changeable things, and present your minds, souls, and spirits to the Lord; and there the seed comes up which is heir of the power, and of the wisdom which is pure from above... And your growth in the seed is in the silence, where ye may all find a feeding of the bread of life. (Fox, Epistle 171)

* * *

Holiness, sanctification

These words can be scary for modern Friends.[16] They carry overtones with which we are uncomfortable. Other words akin to them also feel difficult to say, and especially to apply to ourselves, even as goals toward which to strive—righteousness, purity, perfection, holiness. Yet from the beginning of the Quaker movement, sanctification, perfection, and righteousness

---

16 Here may be a good place to point out that language changes over time; the denotations and connotations of a word may be different in significant ways from one era to the next. Some words which are subject to theological debate, such as "sanctification" or even "light" (is this light natural or divine?) may carry implications to seventeenth-century ears that twenty-first century readers may not notice. Other words, which are theologically rich, but not the subject of internal debates among Friends, may be passed on with fairly consistent meaning within a community, unburdened by outside contrasts. To some extent, the constant relating of our language to our experience of God is also a force for coherence—if the language helps the community interpret its experience in unifying ways.

were seen clearly and freshly as the direction in which the Light leads, and can prepare us for, in our measure. As Fox and his companions were fond of saying, God wishes to save us *from* sin, not to save us *in* sin, leaving us hardly changed at all except in the outward.

These difficult terms are deeply rooted in Scriptural language, both in the Hebrew scriptures (especially the prophets and Psalms, which Friends have loved) and in the Greek scriptures (the New Testament). Friends traditionally have been thoroughly conversant with the scriptures, and, like other Christians, have used biblical language to make sense of their experience. Over the past several decades, however, modern Friends have acquired new ways to describe and understand spiritual experiences, especially using the language of psychology and science. This new language, and the understandings of life that it expresses, mean that we inhabit a very different spiritual world from that of our Friends in the past.

Let us acknowledge that our culture, and our cultural tools and habits of mind, are different from those of Fox or Elizabeth Fry, or even Rufus Jones. As we reflect on our journeys across the inward landscape, we may nevertheless feel our way to a place where the truth of the older language of *sin* and *sanctification* can be allied with our modern language about the self, the community, and the transpersonal. When we reach that place, we can then reckon with the challenge of righteousness and the process of sanctification as a result of the inward work of Christ through the Light, and as a necessary pre-requisite for service to God and God's children.

We might start with a basic element of holiness that we often overlook (perhaps in our anxiety in confronting the invitation to transformation?): consecration or dedication to God. This is nicely summed up in a line from the prophet Zechariah, in which even the most mundane things, when the day of the Lord comes, will be dedicated, or set aside, for use according to the king's (God's) will: "In that day shall there be upon the bells of the horses, HOLINESS UNTO THE LORD" (Zechariah 14:20).

One can more easily imagine—or claim—a dedication, a longing or hoping to be of worthy use, than one can hope for complete perfection, or full spiritual growth. But this is a first step, an evidence that the collaboration or co-creation has begun, under the invitation and first motion of the Spirit of love: "Lord, I believe; help thou mine unbelief!" (Mark 9:24). It is making oneself open, or available, to God, whose fullness longs to unfold

45

itself in and through our personality, changing it and making it ever more hospitable and transparent to the light, the seed, Christ. The idea of *availability* (what Brother Roger of the Taizé community called *disponabilité*, "being at God's disposal") may be an easier way for us to understand and accept the calling to holiness. From that point of view, we can examine why and how we may be unavailable—and see from a fresh perspective the cast-off or alien notions of *sin* that rise up quickly alongside *holiness*.

Much of what was meant by *sinfulness* in the old Quaker language includes the many ways that our bodies, relationships, habits, and hastiness make us unreceptive or inattentive to the gentle motions of the Light. Hicks, Scott, and others described their strong inclinations when young to frivolity, jolly company, and jesting. The eminent Philadelphia minister Rebecca Jones was known in her teens as "Romping Beck." As these increasingly concerned Friends passed into their middle years, their journals less often speak of the temptations of youthful "animal spirits," but rather of pride, over-involvement in work, self-indulgence, anger, stubbornness, or discouragement.[17]

Most of us would not call such faults and distractions from the sense of the Presence of God *sin*. The word *sin* carries with it implications of danger to the immortal soul, and to die in sin, in most eras of Christianity and of early Quakerism, is to die deserving of lasting punishment in the next life, mitigated only by the mercy of God. Modern people, including modern Friends, prefer not to dwell on the long-term effects of distraction, persistent ill-doing, spiritual indifference, and persistent unavailability to God's promptings and the condition of those we meet. Yet when we sit in the quiet presence, and reflect in the Light on our condition, we may come to feel a discouragement or self-rebuke that Woolman or his contemporaries would have recognized. Seeing in the Light the contrast between ourselves as we are, and ourselves as God invites us to be, can provoke even a kind of disgust. Stubborn alienation from the Light, whether we call it sin or not, feels, in those clearest moments, to be really a kind of unhealth

---

17 Though not all. In some of the franker journalists, temptations of an earthier sort remain a challenge. Among many similar entries, Dr. John Rutty writes, "Fawning to superiors, insulting to inferiors: Lord, cleanse from this baseness!" (29), or "Drinking beyond the holy bounds embitters my retrospection, and stains my virtues... Choler with cause in the morning, and without cause in the evening" (52).

or unwholesomeness that we may long to escape, at least while we are able to perceive it.[18]

A response that reaches toward spiritual health consists in our openness to the Inward Teacher and Guide. As we allow the Light to search further and further through our motives, judgments, and commitments, way opens to a resulting gradual change of behavior. While few of us may dare to claim for ourselves that we are growing into holiness, it is possible to recognize with joy (and relief) that some such work has begun in us, and that we have been visited by motions of compassion, courage, and care for the welfare of others. The path to holiness, which is to make ourselves more and more available to God, can become an intentional journey. Our wills and desires can become tools for the discovery and establishment of our new selves in God, where once they were barriers and burdens to the Seed.

Knowing this, tasting it, and seeing it in others, Friends have from the beginning maintained that God's will is for friendship with us, as Jesus proclaimed in the passage of John's Gospel from which Friends take their name: "Henceforth I call you not servants but friends..." (15:15). As we accept this, we find ourselves on a path to complete faithfulness—a perfection that is not a blissful, static end-state, but a growing creation. As God accepts our hospitality and intention, this unfolding process sets about changing everything in our spiritual house. Friends from many backgrounds, and traveling many different paths, have known from vivid personal experience (experimentally, Fox would say) that the Spirit of Christ is at work in each of us, fitting whoever accepts the invitation to bear his mild yoke (Matthew 11:30). We can find a rest for our souls, a place of stability, that persists in the most active and involved life. Perhaps a modern word that best fits, and which can help us unite with the older term "sanctification," is *transformation*.

---

18 Rebecca Jones, at the same time elders might have called her "Romping Beck," was secretly undergoing a deep seeking and transformation of personality, which only surfaced when she shyly confessed it to a minister visiting from a distance. No one in her community suspected what was in the works. See *Biographical Sketches and anecdotes of members of the Religious Society of Friends.* (Philadelphia: The Tract Association of Friends, 1870), 80-81.

Measure

From the beginning of the Quaker movement, it was clear that the Light carries out its work uniquely in each person, and its tempo is shaped by the work of the Spirit and the individual's response. Friends testified from the beginning about the work of rebirth and transformation:

> ...the Lord did gently lead me along, and did let me see his love, which was endless and eternal, and surpasseth all the knowledge that men have in the natural state, or can get by history or books; and that love let me see myself, as I was without him. And I was afraid of all company, for I saw them perfectly, where they were, through the love of God which let me see myself. (Fox, *Journal* 11)

This gentle leading allows the soul to, as it were, increase in capacity, so as to accommodate the new understanding, and not be cast into a sense of helplessness or despair that we might ever come to experience the paradise that occurs when Christ reigns in the heart.

> Nor do I say, that all my sins, which formerly I had committed, of which I had been convinced by the light of the world, when I was in the world, before I believed it to be sufficient, that they were wholly taken away, as my sins of ignorance were; for this I found, that God in this was just and merciful: merciful, in that He did not lay them all at once before me, lest they should have pressed me down, that I could not have followed the light, nor gotten any strength; but must needs have perished under them, had He not spared. And just I have found Him also; for as they were not committed all at once, against the light of His Spirit; so He has at one time or another visited for them, and laid them before me; yet not all at once, nor no way so heavy as those committed after I believed, and gave up myself to follow the light, and yet to an account He has brought me for them. (Nayler 4: 70)

The first movements of the Light can be so small as to feel negligible, and it is tempting in a time of active spiritual growth to be impatient, to want to be more fully mature than we have actually grown to (or worse, to be seen as more fully grown than we are). Hence Friends from the beginning of their spiritual experimentation have reminded each other of the importance of staying with the Guide.

> take heed of that nature that would know more than God is willing to reveal: for you shall find that unwilling to obey what it knows: and take heed of that which desires to appear before men to be commended, for that seldom deserves praise of God. (Nayler 1: 266)

We are to live fully in what we have been led to, and to practice the faithfulness we can be consistent in. This allows us to walk steadily with the Guide:

> All Saints and Children of the Most High God, abide with God in the calling whereunto you are called, which calling is the measure of the Light given unto you... All in your measure, as you have received of the Lord, walk faithfully with him, so will you be preserved pure, clean and unblamable before him, and will be fortified by the Arm of his eternal power, against all the deceit, subtility, windings and twistings of the Serpent within you, and without you. I charge you all in the presence of the Lord God, to abide with God in what he hath communicated to you, and run not out from the Witness of the eternal Spirit, that hath sealed you up in measure in the Power of his love. (Dewsbury 21)

We have been exhorted to steadfastly live out what we have been given, until we are clearly led to something new, since gospel times (see Matthew 20). This can present us with problems in community, when we are tempted to see others' gifts as more valuable or more advanced than ours (as in Romans 14). Yet if we can stay faithful just as far as we are led, and avoid claiming insight that we have not attained to, the variety of gifts and insights within the community can teach us, inspire us, and reassure us. We can give thanks that we know other seekers and finders who occupy many conditions:

> Although some things which others clearly see the necessity of, may not yet be clear to thee, yet the same power which has shown thee some things, can show thee many more if he pleases. Therefore, be careful, and not be too hasty in judging that things are unnecessary, because thou hast not yet seen them; or else, thou mayst condemn the living experience of many who have known far more of the love of God, and of his requirings, than thyself. (Scott, *Works* 2: 11)

The notion of *measure* and of *perfection*, as Friends have understood it, come together as a challenging yet compassionate doctrine, in which we are assured that "it is your Father's good pleasure to give you the kingdom" (Luke 12:32). Yet we are admonished to "be ... perfect as your Father ... in Heaven is perfect" (Matthew 5:48)—in love, joy, peace, long-suffering, teachableness, and the doing of good for others.

> Wherefore, let your food be in the life of what you know, and in the power of obedience rejoice, and not in what you know, but cannot live, for the life is the bread for your souls... So let your labor and diligence be in that which presses into the heavenly Being...and hearken in love to that, not in that mind which would save your own lives, nor feed you where you are; but in love to that which separates you from self-life, and changes you into His life whom you wait for from above; so in receiving His commands in that which loves to be like Him in life, your faith works by love: That faith works obedience, quickness and willingness, it works out the old, and works into the new... (Nayler 4: 155)

Truth

One of the oldest and best-loved queries goes, "How does Truth prosper among you?" This signals clearly that *Truth* is not a set of propositions or doctrines to be asserted, refined, or debated in the light of reason alone. When Jesus said, "And ye shall know the truth, and the truth will make you free" (John 8:32), the freedom he speaks of is freedom into fuller life, and a greater ability to act on one's understanding of God's will. Since body, soul, and mind are always engaged in human life, there are things that Friends assert to be true, but there is no complete collection of "truths" whose sum equals "Truth," as Friends have understood it.

At first glance, the word *Truth* (with a capital T), as Quakers used it, would seem to be a euphemism for God. It is sometimes possible to substitute the word *God* for *Truth* in the writings of Woolman or other Friends without significantly changing the meaning. However, a careful reading reveals that, for the first Quakers, the meaning of Truth expanded far beyond the simple concept of God. It is almost as if Fox and early Quakers remembered and incorporated other connotations of the powerful word *Truth* that go back as far as Wycliffe and Chaucer, and even earlier. For them, Truth seems also to have signified a spiritual reality that was not only just as real as reality, but also incorporated, sustained, and given meaning to all material things. This Truth was not just a doctrine to be believed with the mind and to be assented to with the mouth—it was a reality to be entered by the one who was ready. Traditional Quakers—and John Woolman was certainly strong on this point — knew from their own experience that one does not enter this realm of reality lightly or without cost, for one could not enter or stay there without, as John Woolman put it, "following the dictates of Truth" (95) in all areas of life and "in the management of my outward affairs" (31).

Those who enter into this Truth, this reality, come to feel a sense of the divine harmony that holds our universe together and that operates in our own minds, bodies, and human society. A person who is *in the Truth* can be expected to act in harmony with the laws of what Woolman calls "universal righteousness." To *be in the Truth*, then, means that one can—and will—live out those standards of inward peace through outward gentleness, tenderness to all creatures, and the right and just ordering of human society exemplified by the life and teachings of Jesus.

Truth as an experience, not an assertion or philosophical demonstration, is at the root of Friends testimonies, which are not solutions for social problems, nor positions we adopt in solidarity with other Friends. Testimonies are enactments of the Truth in which we stand: as far as we can understand God's will and God's nature realized in our lives, we are compelled by that will and that life to act in *this* way and not another. Thus Woolman could say that his service among the Indians was first a motion of love, and then a concern to live among them and learn about their life — and that the Indians might possibly be helped by his following the promptings of Truth among them.[19]

It is for this reason that Friends have felt that clearness for membership in a meeting should be reflected in the adoption of some, at least, of the central testimonies held by the meeting. If the person has changed so that this behavior is natural and in a sense unavoidable, this is some evidence that he or she is animated by the common divine life flowing through the community.

The operation of the Light results in a thorough restructuring of a person's worldview and values. Priorities are so changed that the things that hold one in this living Truth, and deepen an establishment in it, become a growing source of challenge, but also of delight. As we noted above, George Fox told how, after his breakthrough encounter with Christ, all creation gave forth a new smell. One can, rooted in this life, even feel that time itself flows differently, and there is a sense of peace even in the most active of lives.[20] This transformation of priorities and perceptions, which Bucke calls a shift in "cosmic consciousness," is a condition in which a ruling principle is compassion. This condition, as John Woolman said, is one where to turn ourselves and all we possess into the channel of universal love, which becomes the chief business of our lives. We long for, and sometimes reflect in our measure, the beauty of holiness.

---

19 The active, concrete nature of Truth as Friends understand it is also embodied, as we see in the old humorous term, *Truth's horses*, referring to the horses kept by a meeting for the use of Friends traveling in the ministry. See Hannah Whitall Smith, *The unselfishness of God: A spiritual autobiography* (New York: Fleming H. Revell Company, 1903, 55.

20 Hugh Barbour comments in a personal communication: "Fox's New Smell may really mean 'Open Eyes for the River from the throne.' "—a radical re-visioning or reorientation. See also Nuttall's essay 'Unity with creation: George Fox and the Hermetic philosophy. in Nuttall, G. 1967. *The Puritan Spirit*. London: Epworth Press. pp 194-203.

IV

The Cross of Joy and the Inward Work of Christ

The Cross is a central symbol of Christianity. It is meaningful and precious to many, including Friends. Because of evil committed in Christ's name, however, the Cross is for some a source of pain and anger, and for others it brings to mind both positive and negative associations. We are aware of how, since Constantine's conversion, the cross has been used as a flag of war and state power, through the Crusades and down to our time. The Cross and Jesus' crucifixion have justified centuries of antisemitism, and many other kinds of oppression, license, and Christian triumphalism, even to the present day.[21]

This sad legacy has been noted by Christians for centuries. John Woolman reports in his journal a dream that conveys something of the burden and complexity of the symbol.[22] The following is an excerpt:

---

21 See James Carroll, Constantine's sword: The Church and the Jews, a history. New York: Houghton Mifflin Company, 2001.

22 The entire dream (pp. 185-6) encapsulates much of the Quaker experience of the work of Christ, in very Pauline language:

In a time of sickness, a little more than two years and a half ago, I was brought so near the gates of death that I forgot my name. Being then desirous to know who I was, I saw a mass of matter of a dull gloomy color between the south and the east, and was informed that this mass was human beings in as great misery as they could be, and live, and that I was mixed with them, and that henceforth I might not consider myself as a distinct or separate being. In this state I remained several hours. I then heard a soft melodious voice, more pure and harmonious than any I had heard with my ears before; I believed it was the voice of an angel who spake to the other angels; the words were, "John Woolman

> I was then carried in spirit to the mines where poor oppressed people were digging rich treasures for those called Christians, and heard them blaspheme the name of Christ, at which I was grieved, for his name to me was precious. I was then informed that these heathens were told that those who oppressed them were the followers of Christ, and they said among themselves, "If Christ directed them to use us in this sort, then Christ is a cruel tyrant." (185-86)

Fox also wrote that Christians do more to turn people away from Christ than any "heathen" could, and all who claim to be Christ's followers would do well to reckon with this truth in humility.

In our times, many (including some Friends) have come rather to a state of indifference in the Cross and its meanings,[23] moving into what has been called a post-Christian stance. In this view, traditional Christianity, and even the doctrines of Christianity as traditionally held by Friends, are largely not relevant, nor part of a living expression of religious experience. This renders the deep, creative Christianity of the Quaker tradition (both of

---

is dead." I soon remembered that I was once John Woolman, and being assured that I was alive in the body, I greatly wondered what that heavenly voice could mean. I believed beyond doubting that it was the voice of an holy angel, but as yet it was a mystery to me.

I was then carried in spirit to the mines where poor oppressed people were digging rich treasures for those called Christians, and heard them blaspheme the name of Christ, at which I was grieved, for his name to me was precious. I was then informed that these heathens were told that those who oppressed them were the followers of Christ, and they said among themselves, "If Christ directed them to use us in this sort, then Christ is a cruel tyrant."

All this time the song of the angel remained a mystery; and in the morning, my dear wife and some others coming to my bedside, I asked them if they knew who I was, and they telling me I was John Woolman, thought I was light-headed, for I told them not what the angel said, nor was I disposed to talk much to any one, but was very desirous to get so deep that I might understand this mystery.

My tongue was often so dry that I could not speak till I had moved it about and gathered some moisture, and as I lay still for a time I at length felt a Divine power prepare my mouth that I could speak, and I then said, "I am crucified with Christ, nevertheless I live; yet not I, but Christ liveth in me. And the life which I now live in the flesh I live by the faith of the Son of God, who loved me and gave himself for me." Then the mystery was opened and I perceived there was joy in heaven over a sinner who had repented, and that the language "John Woolman is dead," meant no more than the death of my own will.

23 See Pink Dandelion, *A sociological analysis of the theology of Quakers: The silent revolution.* Lampeter: Edwin Mellen Press, 1996.

the first 250 years of the movement, and of the majority of those who claim the name *Quaker* today around the world) to some extent inaccessible.

Despite many reasons for rejecting Cross language, however, we believe that this remains a vital concept for Quakerism and not only for historical reasons. Indeed, the work that Friends can do to re-inhabit this language, drawing on the insights of Quaker experience of the living spirit of Christ, can be an important gift to Christianity, and to the ministry of reconciliation within Christendom, as well as between Christians and non-Christians. When one reads the journals and epistles of Friends from the early and middle periods, one sees that, as with other Christian language, early Friends, and those of the middle period, understood the Cross and the crucifixion in a very different way from mainstream Christianity. Just as with *Truth*, as we saw in the previous chapter, the *Cross* for Friends has been experienced as a place, a process, and a state of being that is full of joy and power. For this reason, exploring the Quaker "inward landscape" can help modern Friends refresh their understanding of the Cross images, and feel where there is still abundant life in them.

This is a good place to stop and reflect for a little while about your own associations with the Cross.

- When you think of the Cross, what do you see, what images come to mind? Can you find an early memory of the cross from your childhood?

- Can you remember a time when you began to have questions about the Cross, perhaps as a symbol, or as an element of theology? Can you be in touch with your emotional response?

- Has the Cross been a useful symbol for you? If so, in what ways? Have you seen ways in which it was useful to others?

- Has the Cross been harmful to you? If so, in what ways? Do these wounds remain open, or have you found healing?

- As you consider the Cross as a place or process, how does this understanding fit in with your previous experiences?

The Quaker experience of the Cross

Friends have most often spoken of "being in the Cross" or "dwelling in the Cross." As with the work of Christ, the Cross is not only a historical event with present consequences, but a present, personal experience. George Fox equated it with God's active work: "Though it never be so much to your advantage, deny yourselves and live in the Cross of Christ, the Power of God, for that destroys injustice" (Epistle 200). He also wrote:

> The cross is to the carnal part, which is the ground of images, the ground of the seducers, and the ground of the false prophet... the cross is to that ground, to the root and life of it. This being minded, which is pure and eternal, it makes a separation from all other lovers, and brings to God, and the ground of evil thoughts comes to be opened, and the cross is to that ground; which Cross overturns the world in the heart. Which Cross must be taken up by all who follow Jesus Christ ...Where the world is standing, the Cross is not lived in. But dwelling in the Cross to the world, here the Love of God is shed abroad in the heart, and the Way is opened in the inheritance, which fades not away." (Epistle 51)

> For those who are come to the Light ... and believe in it, they feel the Power of God, they feel Christ and his Cross, which is the Power of God. (Epistle 100)

This cross, then, is the power of God at work in us to transform us into Children of the Light, revealing the contrasts between a life lived in that Light, and our lives untouched by it. When Fox says, "the Cross is to [some evil or failing]," he means that the life and Power of God rejects the evil or failing, and if we mind that power, we can receive the healing and transformation.[24] Sometimes Friends used phrases like "It was in the cross to me" to mean, "I had to struggle against my inclinations, peer pressure,

---

24 Recall Nayler, in his "Last Testimony": "There is a spirit which I feel, that delights to do no evil, nor to revenge any wrong, but delights to endure all things, in hope to enjoy its own in the end. Its hope is to outlive all wrath and contention, and to weary out all exaltation and cruelty, or whatever is of a nature contrary to itself." (Works 4: 382)

or my own personality, in order to take this step of faithfulness." Yet to take such a difficult step (however trivial it might seem to someone else) is an integral part of taking up our daily Cross in following Jesus into the immense love of God, who can enable us to lay down our lives, most often in our daily faithfulness, for the love of God and our neighbor.

So we need to keep dwelling in the Cross, that is, to stay steadfastly aware, available, and responsive to the love and light of God, since there are so many opportunities to forget and grow spiritually cold. John Woolman described this process with quiet delight in his journal:

> As I lived under the cross, and simply followed the openings of Truth, my mind from day to day was more enlightened; my former acquaintance was left to judge of me as they would, for I found it safest for me to live in private and keep these things sealed up in my own breast.
>
> While I silently ponder on that change wrought in me, I find no language equal to it nor any means to convey to another a clear idea of it. I looked upon the works of God in this visible creation and an awefulness covered me; my heart was tender and often contrite, and a universal love to my fellow creatures increased in me. This will be understood by such who have trodden in the same path. Some glances of real beauty may be seen in their faces who dwell in true meekness. There is a harmony in the sound of that voice to which divine love gives utterance, and some appearance of right order in their temper and conduct whose passions are fully regulated. Yet all these do not fully show forth that inward life to such who have not felt it, but this white stone and new name [cf. Rev. 2:17] is known rightly to such only who have it. (28-29)

Indeed, here we come to the paradox expressed in the title of this chapter, the Cross of Joy. As Woolman describes, and many other Friends can testify, when we participate in the transformational work of the Light, accepting the truth it reveals, and as power comes, and we move into the greater faithfulness, there comes a sense of enlargement in freedom and in love that is not a reward for good behavior, but an increase in well-being that opens us to joy, because we have been healed in some way. We may experience at first struggle, disorientation, or deprivation — a straitened path — yet it sets the stage for a new birth through which the divine life has greater, more welcome scope in our personality and outlook. After some experience of this transformation process, we can come to embrace it when we feel it happening, knowing that it leads to joy, often in unexpected forms.[25]

Bill Taber sometimes was led to describe a particular time in which his experience of the Cross was especially vivid and life-changing, and to reflect on the consequences that he felt and experienced as a result.

Bill's experience of the Cross of Joy

"It happened to me on New Year's Eve a few hours before the year 1965. I was then a second-year student at Earlham School of Religion, spending part of the holidays with my wife and small daughter at my wife's parents. For some reason, I felt led to skip supper that evening and take a small cup of yogurt up to an upstairs room to consider what God might be asking of me for the year to come.

"For a time, I pondered and wrote in my journal, considering the year past and the year to come. Then I waited. I don't know how long I waited, but eventually I was surprised by what I can only call an awareness of the Cross of Joy. I was surprised because I had expected that God would ask some great sacrifice, some great task in the year to come. Instead of the great Christian heroics that I thought God wanted of me, I gradually realized that He simply wanted me to accept whatever happened to me in the spirit of the Cross of Joy. As I gradually absorbed this amazing fact, I became aware of the radiant love of God: patient, tender, uplifting, and healing, as manifested through Jesus Christ. Of course, there would be work for me to do in the year to come, but God was asking me to pay attention to the special attitude with which I did that work. The tenderness of God the Father was encouraging me to accept every event—good, bad, or

---

25 This paradox is known to Christians in many times and places, although with differing nuances. Here is Julian of Norwich: "I was very joyful; I understood that in our Lord's intention we are now on his cross with him in our pains, and in our sufferings we are dying, and with his help and his grace we willingly endure on that same cross ... Suddenly he will change his appearance for us ... and then all will be brought into joy" (*Showings*, 9th revelation, 21st chapter).

indifferent—with the quiet joy of one who knows that God, who is good, is always present in every event, every phenomenon.

"On that New Year's Eve thirty-seven years ago, I did not fully understand all of the intellectual and theological implications of that experience, but I did try to remember it in my work at Earlham School of Religion, my weekend work at Marion First Friends Meeting, and my work with interracial dialog in Richmond [Indiana]. One example of practicing the Cross of Joy early in that year still remains fresh in my memory. It happened one night, when I was driving from Richmond to an adult Sunday School gathering in Marion, where I was serving as intern pastor. I was in a hurry because I was already late. Suddenly I realized that I had a flat tire. It was dark, cold, and there was snow on the ground. I quickly pulled off the country road, beside a house that had a good yard light, so I could see enough to change the tire. Because of my memory of the Cross of Joy, what could have been a time of irritation, frustration, and feeling sorry for myself became a time of quiet and joyous acceptance. I can still remember feeling and actually enjoying the cold snow, the touch of cold metal and the brisk air in my lungs as I changed the tire. Because I accepted the flat tire in the Cross of Joy, I was fully present and I felt amazingly alive and at peace inwardly, even though I was late."

Reflecting on the vision in the years since

Bill continues: "I wish I could say that I continued to experience that attitude of sacred acceptance in every moment through the rest of that year, as well as during the rest of my life. Many times I have forgotten, but the New Year's memory has served as a reminder and a compass needle for the journey of my soul.

"Over the years I have come to realize that many Christian spiritual teachers recommend this way of being totally present—and accepting—in all circumstances. They have many ways of describing it. Thomas Kelly, for example, speaks of this attitude as 'everything matters—nothing matters.' These teachers are not telling us not to care when there is disaster, evil, pain—they encourage us to care deeply in fellowship with the compassionate Christ. When we stay focused on God in all circumstances, our minds and our wills are much clearer, so that we are more free to choose—and do—what is best in that situation. Paradoxically, the more we can keep our focus on God, or on Jesus, the more we are able, at the same time, to be fully present to the situation or the person before us. Sometimes, what we might at first think of as a disaster turns out not to be that at all, as we accept it in the Cross of Joy....

"The Cross of Joy does not always abolish pain. It simply makes it possible for each of us to bear the pain as well as the good fortune in each of our lives, without being distracted either by the pain or the fame. However, when we live with this attitude, this state of consciousness, we often discover that we are more free to learn how God would have us change our way of thinking or our behavior in order to ease our pain or the pain of others. Jesus, of course, knew the Cross of Joy. Only because he lived it so fully was He able to bear that other cross and to bear with infinite love the incredible burden of humanity, which He bears to this moment, sustaining you and me....

"A well-known passage from Romans 8:28 (RSV) is, 'We know that in everything God works for good with those who love him, who are called according to His purpose.' Here, the Apostle Paul is not saying that all things are good. He is not saying that accidents, illness, untimely death or acts of violence are good—only that God is present and at work in all circumstances, opening a way for some good to occur out of even the worst situations. As we live in the Cross of Joy, we can stay open to this work of God in ourselves and others, even in difficult and grieving times. People for whom this passage is a lifeline usually pay close attention to its two requirements.

"The first is that 'God works for good with those who *love* him.' If we seriously seek to hold on to the promise of Romans 8:28, we need to ponder what it means to really love the Lord. We all know how easy it is say that we love the Lord without paying attention to the moment-by-moment attitude, behavior, and lifestyle, which such love requires.

"The second requirement is that 'God works for good for those ... who are called according to his purpose.' In other words, God works for good in all situations if we stay alert to what He is asking us to be and do in that moment, as well as in the rest of our lives. The very next verse suggests that our real calling is 'to become like His Son, so that His Son would be the first born, with many brothers and sisters.' Thus, the promise of Romans

8:28 is calling each of us to become like Jesus, to live in the Cross of Joy as He did, and to spread his message and His Spirit in whatever unique way He leads us."

Living in the Cross of Joy as a state of awareness

Bill continues: "The writings of our spiritual forbear, George Fox, often tell us to 'keep in the daily cross, the power of God.' When Fox spoke of living in the cross, for example in epistles 51 and 150, he often said that living in the cross is 'the power of God.' In other words, we cannot know the life and power that Fox experienced without living in that attitude or the state of mind of the 'the inward cross.' Fox is not alone in this reminder to 'live in the cross.' Quaker journalists across three centuries have many references to their experience of living in the cross, or being in the cross. When I am with modern liberal Friends who are reluctant to use Christian terminology, I love to open up the powerful meaning of Fox's admonition to live in the cross by suggesting that he is talking about a state of mind, or a level of consciousness, that may be akin to what the Buddhists mean by nonattachment. In other words, living in the cross is, first of all, being keenly alert to the highest reality we know, in every moment, so that we are able to choose, microsecond by microsecond, the attitude and action most in line with the will of God. Living in the cross is akin to 'nonattachment' because in this state of alertness we can be given the grace and the self-discipline to give up our own will, our own attachments, and our own prejudices through the incredible grace of God manifested through Jesus Christ.

"Living in the Cross of Joy is not a one-time experience. It is life-long and is an important symbol of soul's journey in this earthly life. Most of us keep learning throughout our lives about what this cross really requires in terms of personal growth and personal change. I have never yet met a mature Christian who did not admit to having had to—at least occasionally—learn new dimensions or subtleties about living in the cross on the daily walk with Jesus... The Cross of Joy teaches us that we can humbly learn the new lesson in the confidence given us in Romans 8:28. All we need to do is look around us in our meetings to usually see—or at least remember—someone whose very presence and behavior are radiant with the peace and love of Christ, because they have learned to live in the Cross of Joy.

"Living in the Cross of Joy opens our eyes to see ourselves more clearly, with 'non- attachment.' Just as Jesus in the gospels restored sight to the blind, so He now gives us new eyes to see ourselves more nearly as God would have us see. For some, this comes as an awesome revelation, as it did to early Friends who spoke of being convicted as the light of Christ revealed how much of them needed to be changed. For most of us, this clearer vision comes in incremental awarenesses so that we can learn—and practice—one new step at a time.

"With this sharper vision, we come to understand more clearly what Christian spiritual teachers and the New Testament say about the self—the egocentric and individualist self—which they all tell us must die and be transformed. In moments of conversion and commitment, we can make great strides through the grace of Christ in this transformation of the old self. Yet, I believe that for most Christians, this is only the beginning of a life-long journey of continuing to live in the cross, the Cross of Joy. Since the inspired writers of the New Testament spent so much time on matters of behavior and ethics suggests that many of the early Christians still had something to learn about daily, continuously living in the Cross of Joy.

"George Fox had a wonderful way of describing how Christ brings about this dramatic as well as continual transformation of the self: he called it the *inward work of Christ*. He fully accepted the outward work of Christ, which altered the cosmos and made personal salvation available to ordinary people like you and me. In addition, however, Fox placed great emphasis on the *inward work* of Christ, which, when we really welcome Christ within us, transforms our old self. Fox insisted that we also need to allow, accept, and cooperate with the *inward work* of Christ that transforms us from the inside out, in the spirit of those wonderful passages about the new covenant in Jeremiah 31:33-34 and Ezekiel 36:24-27."

Growing as we live in the Cross of Joy

Bill concludes: "Most of us have probably experienced what might be called 'beginners' grace'— perhaps several times—as I have. It is wonderful how God gives us a foretaste of what the Christ-transformed life can be like. But for most of us, the intensity of the honeymoon ends, and we realize that we are in this relationship with Christ for the long haul. When we stumble and forget, and find ourselves back in some of the patterns, attitudes, and habits of the old self, the memory of the Cross of Joy can help us recover and return to alert faithfulness. It is at this point, during the long haul after the honeymoon (which is where I suspect most of us are), that we can use a little help from experienced Friends. Fortunately, we can turn to spiritual writers, pastors, spiritual friends, and certainly the Bible, to help us stay faithful to the lifelong process of cooperating with the inward work of Christ, transforming us to become ever more like Him."

Bill's reflections conclude

"So, whether we call it 'living in the cross,' or 'remembering the cross of joy,' there is no other way that can bring us inward peace, once we have known the touch of the Living Christ. In the midst of all our work with families, jobs, meetings, and communities, there is always the background music of our relationship with Christ who is leading us safely through the valley of the shadow of death, the death of the old self. Paradoxically, this is not a gruesome business — instead it is health and life and joy. Living in the Cross of Joy does not create somber and sober saints; instead it frees people to be more alive, creative, and vital.

"If we continually seek to live in the Cross of Joy and to share this experience with our spiritual friends and our meetings, we keep ourselves open to that amazing transformation of our old nature through the grace of Jesus Christ. Through this grace, we can live out the Cross of Joy in all of our relationships.

"First of all, we can do it with ourselves, in the secrecy of our inner private world of thoughts, reactions, memories, and emotions, allowing Christ to be the radiant center of our being. If we forget (as I do, many times), the Cross of Joy can bring us back instantly to alert obedience to Christ without wasting time in recrimination or discouragement.

"The Cross of Joy can also enrich family and community life. Jesus Christ is always present in our homes, at our tables, and in our committees, no matter what frustrations or problems may threaten to obscure this reality.

"Living in the Cross of Joy does not make us a passive doormat. The Cross helps us to wait for a microsecond before we respond to a difficult situation, so that our response comes not from the old Adam, but from the ever new and transformed being in Christ. It is as if the Holy Spirit expands time, giving us the amazing grace to be more creative, helpful, and Christian in our response and actions."

V

Varieties of the Inward Motion

The spiritual life is full of incidents, findings and losings, trials, break-throughs, puzzles, and insights. It is no coincidence that we find the words "travail" and "travel" apparently interchangeable in the journals! The language of the inward landscape is rich in descriptions of such events and transitions, as Friends sought to bring a consciousness of divine guidance and presence into every aspect of life — another form of ancient Christian call to "pray without ceasing" (1 Thessalonians 5:17).

Isaac Penington, that poet of inward travels, tells us what to watch for early in our walk in the Light, in language that travels the border between sensory experience (touch, taste, sound, sight) and the ineffable:

> There is a creating, a quickening power in the light, which begets a little life, and that can answer the voice of the living power...Hast thou never found a true, honest breathing towards God? Hast thou never found sin not an imaginary, but a real burden? This was from life: there was somewhat begotten of God in thee, which felt this. It was not the flesh and blood in thee; but somewhat from above... [men's minds] look for some great appearance of power, and so they slight and overlook the day of small things, and neglect receiving the beginning of that, which in the issue would be the thing they look for. Waiting in that which is low and little in the heart, the power enters, the seed grows, the kingdom is felt and daily more and more revealed in the power. And this is the true door and way to the thing: take heed of climbing over it. (1: 125-6)

However we describe it theologically, our awareness of God's nature at work in us, and the way we must (can) live into it in order to claim our heritage as children of God, represents a new sensitivity, a new knowing that does not come from the physical senses, but is experienced and described in several ways:

- as an active guide - the "Inward Monitor" (i.e. watcher and warner), the inward teacher

- as a quality of consciousness: "Best wisdom," "Ancient Wisdom," or "Pure Wisdom"

- as the Mind of Christ

It is apparent from the journals and other writings by Friends of earlier times, as well as from the words of modern Friends, that as one turns towards the Light, and accepts its searching, teaching power, one becomes acutely aware of one's own spiritual condition, and sometimes that of others. As one begins to encounter, even faintly, the sense of divine Presence, one experiences the *tendering*, or becoming tender, that Fox spoke of with such appreciation and frequency.

* * *

Tendering

As we find ourselves coming to the center, the Light becomes perceptible to us. The first operation in this new consciousness is *tendering*. The word *tender* was dear to Fox. He loved to look for tender people, and Friends often spoke of being *tendered* by the power of the Holy Spirit. In modern language, someone is *tender* if they are open to feeling, especially feelings of compassion, love, and pity; Fox and other Quaker writers used the word in this sense. Friends have used this term in referring to regions of the inward landscape, but there are other nuances, which might be summed up as being open to spiritual influence.

Often, however, we must be *made* tender, with our defenses broken down, or our pride disarmed, so that we are malleable, and willing to hear where we are in need of guidance towards a closer walk with the Guide who is both Breaker-in and Mender:

O let us not put off our repentance any longer! but *today, while it is called today, let us hear his voice, and harden not our hearts;* but be of tender heart; let our hearts be softened and tendered under the word of God, and under the strokes of his judgment. If ever the Lord bring you under a tender frame, you will receive the word of God with meekness, and mix it with faith. Then it will work effectually to the amendment of your lives. (Crisp 196)

It is good in trying to understand the word *tender* to remember Isaiah's passages about the clay in the hands of the potter, or the human spirit shaped under the creative work of God's hands. *Tender* in this sense implies that we are available, vulnerable, and receptive to change and transformation (moving towards holiness). A person's actions or words may surprise us, or strike through our defenses or habitual ways of thinking in such a way that we become aware of feelings that we have ignored before. God has been calling, visiting, keeping us company all the time, but we don't always notice and respond. *Staying tender* is another way to talk about the fundamental Quaker experience—dwelling in the Presence, being attuned to the small inward motions of the Spirit, and learning more and more to maintain or return to that awareness throughout the day.

The root of the *tenderness* that we can learn to see and cherish is a reflection of the gentleness, the humility, of the Lord's work and inward appearance in us, "the tender thing":

I went among the professors at Duckinfield and Manchester, where I stayed awhile, and declared truth among them. There were some convinced who received the Lord's teaching, by which they were confirmed and stood in the truth. But the professors were in a rage, all pleading for sin and imperfection, and could not endure to hear talk of perfection, and of a holy and sinless life. But the Lord's power was over all, though they were chained under darkness and sin, which they pleaded for, and quenched the tender thing in them. (Fox, *Journal* 18)

* * *

Feel, Feeling, Feelings

These words have appeared many times already in this book! From the beginning, Friends tried to express their inward experience in terms of *feeling*. They would feel a motion of love; they would feel drawn in gospel love to visit a place; they would feel a stop in the mind. It is important to emphasize that in Quaker parlance such phrases are not describing emotional states, although they often are followed by emotion, or accompanied by it. This particular Quaker sense of *feeling* is a kind of knowing, a moment of clarity on a specific point, a heightened or intensified awareness of a situation, condition, or fact. We can say that when we come to the center where we are able to perceive the divine life, the inward teacher in action; *we have come down to the place that knows*.[26]

George Fox often speaks of feeling as a knowing without words, perhaps even a pre-conscious realization. This is illustrated by a dramatic story from the time of his imprisonment in Cornwall:

> Another time, about eleven at night, the jailer, being half drunk, came and told me that he had got a man now to dispute with me: (this was when we had leave to go a little into the town). As soon as he spoke these words I felt there was mischief intended to my body. All that night and the next day I lay down on a grass-plot to slumber, and felt something still about my body: I started up, and struck at it in the power of the Lord, and still it was about my body.
>
> Then I rose and walked into the Castle-Green, and the under-keeper came and told me that there was a maid would speak with me in the prison. I felt a snare in his words, too, therefore I went not into the prison, but to the grate; and looking in, I saw a man that was lately brought to prison for being a conjurer, who had a naked knife in his hand. I spoke to him, and he threatened to cut my chaps; but, being within the jail he could not come at me. This was the jailer's great disputant. I went soon after into the jailer's house, and found him at breakfast; he had then got his conjurer out with him. I told the jailer his plot was discovered. (*Journal* 256)

---

26 Whittier catches this very well in his poem "The Quaker of the olden time": "He walked by faith and not by sight/By love and not by law;/The presence of the wrong or right/He felt rather than saw."

Later Friends came to talk about *feeling clear*, that is, to understand that one had no further obligation to continue with a task, or to feel that one has no objection to a particular course of action. One might "*feel to* do something," meaning that one is led in a spiritual sense to an action. This understanding of feeling is rooted in the Quaker experience that God's guidance can be perceived, or felt, by the individual in the course of daily life, and that one's life can be (should come to be) shaped by responding to this knowing.

Of course, feelings can have many origins, and we can very well feel certain about something in which we are quite mistaken. This underscores the whole work of discernment, which includes both *feeling* and thinking, often very shrewd thinking. As Hugh Barbour wrote:

> Early Friends faced the daily job of recognizing the true from the subjective when they were led to speech and action. From Jeremiah's time to the present, men have known no absolute or easy way to tell a genuinely divine message from wishful impulses and false prophecy. ("Five Tests," 1)

There are symptoms or guidelines that can help us in this discerning. Even if there is no algorithm that will unfailingly provide the content of the "right answer" when we are seeking clarity, there are ways we can test whether one path leads towards the light (as described above) or away from it. Most of the tests become more reliable, the more acquainted we are with the voice of the Shepherd, and the more experience we have in mistaking our own hopes, fears, or desires for the will of God. Scripture can help, the discipline and practices of our community help, but in the end we must come to an inward equilibrium in which reason and community are only ingredients. We might say that it is the quality of the life that seems to open, under one option or another, that gives us the foundational guidance. Nayler writes:

> It is the like of gentleness, meekness, patience, and all other virtues which are of a springing and spreading nature, where they are not quenched, but suffered to come forth to His praise in His will and

time, who is the Begetter thereof, and to the comfort of His own Seed, and cross to the world. (4: 30)

Wrapped up in Nayler's words are several elements of this life quality: truthfulness, even if in tension with our preferences or our self-image; gentleness, meekness, and comfort; but also a springing and spreading: increased capacity and expansive/outward-reaching action, which have an integrity because they grow from within, and in continuity with the divine Life.

Astute Friends wrote with some asperity of those who, no doubt meaning well, aspired to insight without exercising sufficient discernment or self-examination:

> Dear friends, let those alone who think they fly into the third heavens, and run into high things, great sights, and deep mysteries; yet love them, and seek peace as much as in you lies. And if any are offended at you, because you see not what they pretend to, bear it patiently, for they ought not so to be; the apostle Paul did not so, but became all things to all, seeking to gain all to Christ Jesus; even so do all who abide in the same spirit to this day. (Gratton 354)

We are rightly careful of the language of intuition and sudden insight, and yet if we are honest, we know that this is an important part of a lively internal life. Consciousness can appear like a stream of water, and we tend to dwell at the surface and to notice phenomena there. Very often our interpretations of our own or others' conditions consist of our conjectures and reasonings about what might be causing a ripple, some eddy, or that splash. It may be useful to imagine an experience in which we are sitting by the side of a brook, and noticing that when the wind ruffles the surface, it becomes opaque. We cannot look past the surface down into the water where things may be happening. Yet when the wind dies down, the surface becomes smooth. As we gaze at it, we may first see something like a mirror, showing us only our own image and reflection. Yet if we wait, and the light is just right, we can see past our own image towards the stream bottom, where other kinds of life are going on. The events down there are part of the whole truth of that stream, even though they only sometimes break the surface, yet give the stream its character. An understanding of the stream is far from complete without an understanding of the life beneath the surface.

So it is with our initial encounters in the living stream of the divine life. Much of what we encounter at first is unclear to us, and we may primarily be aware of our emotions, impulses, and thoughts. As we glimpse a power or process at work that we are not in command of, our first reaction may be a sensation of rest or relief, or it may be a feeling of anxiety, perhaps discomfort with the unknown and unscripted. After a while, however, with repeated practice, we learn to allow ourselves to be immersed in that living stream. We can learn new ways to participate in the inward life, along with all other life and souls that share in it.

* * *

Our friend's spiritual language may differ from our own

It may be useful to stop here and to recognize that the language of inward experiences, of inward motions, is not meaningful to everyone as an expression of their experience. There are Friends, and very valuable Friends indeed, who would not claim for themselves a mystical experience in their spiritual lives. John Stephenson Rowntree was one of the most prominent British Friends of the nineteenth century, during the time when an evangelical theology was most in the forefront. He was known as an insightful, tender counselor and minister, both in meeting and in his one-to-one opportunities with persons who were seeking or in need. Yet he never claimed for himself an unmistakable experience of inward guidance. Rather, he "mistrusted the guidance of impulse unless it had the sanction of reason and judgment behind it... that when he was facing a decision, he prayed in faith, and then did what seemed best to him at the time.... [like Missionary Colliard] he was sure that he was guided, but only very rarely was he conscious, at the time, of guidance" (Doncaster 26).

William Littleboy, another British Friend active in the early part of the twentieth century, was moved to write a pamphlet on Quaker experience "for the non-mystic."[27] His own experience was not well expressed by the

---

27 It might be asked whether the language of the inward landscape is in fact "mystical." Littleboy would

language of the inward landscape as he heard it used by the Friends and ministers of his day. This language of feelings, while it has been a powerful and consistent way to speak of inward condition and inward growth for Friends generation after generation, is not a universal language. It may well be that more Friends than we know have not been able to use feeling-language to speak of their own personal experience.

Nevertheless, when Friends have been led to articulate their spiritual experience, this language of feelings, openings, tenderness, "stops," and warmth or coolness, has served to give names to experiences that are not fully expressible in words. As with all vocalization of spiritual matters, such terms are tools, aides, guides, or sometimes reminders. They can never be definitive, however, and so we must be careful as we use these words to describe what is happening too simply or concretely.

* * *

Inward Peace as guide and method

With this caution in mind, we can continue to explore some of the terms Friends have used to describe their growth in the Spirit as they came under the inward work of Christ. Once we make ourselves available to the work of the Light, we embark on a journey across the inward landscape, a journey marked repeatedly by encounters with people, questions, and situations where our spirits are tried and our clarity can be lost for the time being. Our experience with the Light is one of unfolding the growing inward dimension, as one might say, as the Christ-life grows in us. We become transformed into persons with new capacities for love and truth.

At any particular point in our lives, when one is at least for that time in the habit of standing in the Light, one is led to the next step of transformation, the next breakthrough. Such breakthroughs or establishment in the Light are in no sense final or invincible. We may reach a place of some peace, assurance, or rest. But that new rest is not the end of the journey;

---

primarily have had in mind two sorts of mysticism very current in the Quakerism of his time (and ours): the eminent Quaker Rufus Jones's view of mysticism as an unmediated sense of encounter with the Divine; and also the more general, Quietist language of inward sensations, such as we are exploring in this book.

it is a vantage point from which we can see farther or better than we could before. Once our understanding is opened further, our conscience becomes sensitive to things that did not bother us deeply before. Our sense of comfort or peace is then shattered or disturbed by the fresh perception of something that does not seem to comport with the divine life that we have begun to taste and accept for ourselves. When Nayler in his so-called "dying words" tried to describe the spirit in which he found himself, he said that "its hope is to outlive all wrath and contention, and to weary out all exaltation and cruelty, or whatever is of a nature contrary to itself" (4: 382). And so we find that standing in the Light and enjoying the sense of blessing that attends our journey, we come to see with fresh insight and courage that there is some other aspect of ourselves whose nature is contrary to the Light. For example, John Woolman wrote of a time when a local person of good reputation came to have Woolman write his will, and part of the man's property consisted of "young Negroes." Woolman said, "I cannot write thy will without breaking my own peace," and could not in conscience proceed. This witness led eventually to the man's arranging for the slaves to be freed. Woolman recounted the incident as one step in a long story of growth (50-1).

It is also important at such times of new clarity and freedom to receive the joy of it, although soberly, knowing that there is no guarantee of invulnerability if our watchfulness (what moderns might call mindfulness) falters. An unexpected trial, a surge of busyness at our work or in family life—or meeting activity—may distract and distance us. Spiritual writers across the ages warn us that even very gifted and passionate souls can find themselves growing cold and out of touch with the sense of the divine presence. The factors that can lead us this way are evident enough, but whether through inattention, or unwillingness to act on a leading, or the cares and demands of life, one's watch slumbers, one's ear is dulled, and the habit of mindfulness is lost.

If you become aware that this has happened, or that you now see something in yourself contrary to the Light, do not lay violent hands on yourself, trying to solve the problem by "will power," or waste time in self-reproach. God who calls us, and reveals our condition, is present to strive with us until the distance between God and God's child is bridged, the barrier overcome:

> [the Lamb] having kindled the fire and awakened the creature, and broken their peace and rest in sin, he waits in patience to prevail ....wrestling with God against the enmity, with prayers and tears night and day, with fasting, mourning and lamentation, in patience, in faithfulness, in truth, in love unfeigned, in longsuffering, and in all the fruits of the Spirit, that if by any means he may overcome evil with good. (Nayler 4: 4)

Once you feel the loss, and the disquiet or grief of it, just start, as if from the beginning, to set aside a little time of quiet and attention. The meditation masters tell us that if one's attention wanders, one should just gently return to the center, as often as necessary. In the same way, when one realizes that one is in a time of coolness, one should directly, but without alarm, take up whatever practice is possible, and with confidence await refreshment and power. Simple is safest.

The reader might be forgiven for thinking that what we are describing is first and foremost an inward-referencing, self-referencing growth, but all the varieties of experience—work, family, citizenship, commerce, art—can motivate further spiritual growth, further exploration and experience of the inward landscape. Recall the passage in George Fox's *Journal*, during his early time of seeking and finding, when he came to the city of Litchfield and saw the steeple house there, the spires of the cathedral, and he wrote, "they struck at my life" (71). His peace was disturbed by an outward circumstance that carried great meaning for him in his tendered state, and then he was impelled to a kind of witness he had never made before. His pain and seeking were not driven by an intellectual dilemma, but by a hunger for integrity in life, worship, and action. A particular concrete circumstance—seeing the church building—was a reminder and renewal of this challenge. Similarly, when John Woolman first resisted or objected to the institution of slavery, it was occasioned by a request to participate personally in the legal transfer of human property from one master to his heirs. This external request focused his understanding and intensified his discomfort. Woolman recognized that the act of writing the will would alienate him from the Light as he had received it. So he sought in all humility for the inward resource to act on this understanding.

Of course, sometimes our peace is indeed disturbed because of an inward realization about our own condition that leaves us with a sense of dissatisfaction. We may come to see that we are too much distracted, or "cumbered," by the affairs of the world in which we are involved, as John Woolman and many other Friends have experienced. We find ourselves distracted by our duties, our commitments, our pleasures, our relationships. Our peace is shattered because we find ourselves out of reach of the light we long for, and we miss the sense of sweetness that comes with a recognition of divine presence in our daily lives, even if often it is in the background.

One may also come to see that anger, lack of discipline, or some other negative emotion is corroding some relationship that we have, or that we find ourselves complicit in some situation that we can no longer tolerate and retain the peace that we have known before. Such realizations can be gentle and gradual; sometimes they can be urgent, disturbing, or distracting; and the way they strike us may vary according to our personalities.

Day in and day out, moment by moment, one learns to attune one's attention to the place, not far from the stream of divine life, where the soul can recognize and admit its need. We are spiritually satisfied by God's life, and without it we are poor and restless. Every day we can benefit from Isaac Penington's challenge to see our condition truly, and to reject counterfeit confidence:

Now to the soul that hath felt breathings towards the Lord formerly... I have this to say: Where art thou? Art thou in thy soul's rest? Dost thou feel the virtue and power of the gospel? Dost thou feel the ease which comes from the living arm, to the heart which is joined to it in the light of the gospel? Is thy laboring for life in a good degree at an end? And dost thou feel the life and power flowing in upon thee from the free fountain? Is the load really taken off from thy back? Dost thou find the captive redeemed and set free from the power of sin, and the captivity broken ... by the redeeming power, which is eternal? Hast thou found this, or hast thou missed of it? Let thine heart answer. Ah! do not imagine and talk away the rest and salvation of thy soul. The gospel state is a state of substance, a state of enjoying the life, a state of feeling the presence and power of the Lord in his pure, holy Spirit, a state of binding-up, a state of healing, a state of knowing the Lord, and walking with him in the light of his own Spirit. It begins in a sweet, powerful touch of life, and there is a growth in the life (in the power, in the divine virtue, in the rest, peace, and satisfaction of the soul in God) to be administered and waited for daily. (2: 202-3)

In all these cases, the return of inward peace is the reward of obedience, or the sense that spiritual equilibrium has been restored ("now I can live with myself!"). The return to peace after a struggle to obey is the first and most essential evidence that one has, in fact, understood what God was requiring—even if the obedience brought no other satisfaction.

My mind still felt heavily laden respecting Friends, whom I requested to stop [stay, after meeting] till others had withdrawn; when, through the renewings of best help, I was enabled to leave the burden with them in much plain counsel, as my way opened, and thought I felt quite clear of all ranks; but going home with a friend to dine, as I entered under the roof, my mind became again secretly and painfully exercised, and I found I had something more to do. Being desirous to stand in resignation, I requested the family might be brought together, and endeavoured faithfully to impart such counsel as Truth opened; for which I felt the reward of peace. (Routh 77)

* * *

Being prepared for growth

Friends have had the experience of being prepared for an opening, before the call actually came, or feeling readied for a future service. This has been reported in the journals of ministers, who often had a warning (either from an inward premonition, or a message from another person) that they would be called to speak on behalf of God for the instruction, warning, or comfort of the people. William Dewsbury famously described how he felt moved to preach the Gospel after conscience drove him from Cromwell's army, but also felt inward instruction to wait several years, "until 1652," which turned out to be the year he joined George Fox in the infancy of the Quaker movement. From the 1700s, Sarah Stephenson writes:

> While I was at Liverpool I had a prospect of the awful service of the ministry; and after being awhile at Lancaster, my cousin John Bradford had a sense of it, and mentioned it in a private opportunity. But, I saw myself as such a poor creature, and the work so awfully great, that I did not give up to it during the two years I was there, nor until sore trials made me willing... (174)

As part of such preparation, Friends become more alert to certain kinds of signals, phenomena, news stories, or words as they go through their day. These people may not be able to describe or explain the heightened sense of attention they find in their surroundings or in themselves, until the clarity arrives unexpectedly during a time of prayer, meeting for worship, or in some commonplace activity. They realize that something is missing, or present, that causes them spiritual pain, and they need to name this pain as well as they can, and open themselves to guidance for a response.

It sometimes happens that people find themselves moved towards a greater sense of concern, of a more consistent or challenging practice than they have been in the habit of using, for no reason that they can really articulate. Sometimes this takes the form of a deepening of spiritual practice; sometimes it is centered on some course of action.

Bill Taber loved to tell the story of his friend William Cope, who found himself led in middle life to set aside a time every morning for some devotional reading and quiet prayer. He had no particular purpose in mind except that it felt best to do so. After several months of maintaining this practice, Cope sat down one morning and looked into his heart and, he said, found that someone had been there. The inward growth that had been gathering in this Friend began to permeate his living, so that he was gifted with a sensitive ministry and more tender witness in his community. The sitting in quiet, turning towards prayer, and taking time just to be in the Presence was not done in order to achieve this outcome. As Cope gave in to the sense that he should take up this morning practice, it fed him, or tendered him, and made him more accessible to the work of the Spirit.

A moving story from an Australian Friend provides a different illustration of how expectant waiting can be combined with the sense of yearning or requirement, in preparation for the opening way. Joseph Neave, of Sydney, rose in the yearly meeting session of 1894 to share a "weight" that was on his mind:

> I am convinced that I have a call. There is something I have to do concerning Russia. I have prayed and prayed but I can find no further guidance. I feel it right for me to go to England, and there the way may open up. But I have not the means to do this, or for whatever further I may be called to do. Friends, I lay this matter before you, knowing that only in doing this, can the load be taken from my mind. (Australia Yearly Meeting, 99)

After long waiting, Friends volunteered funds to get Neave to England. There, gradually, the unfocused concern for Russia found its realization in a mission to save members of the Doukhobors, a persecuted pacifist sect, and to help them emigrate to Canada.

Availability

It is good to remember, and this may be especially useful for newcomers to a meeting to hear, that the sensible experience of divine guidance that Friends have held so dear, and suffered for so much, was probably in the majority of cases, day in and day out, not experienced as the receiving of a positive command. Sometimes when we describe what happens in meeting, we will find ourselves saying that we "center down" or "become very quiet and listen for messages from God." And of course this is true. But the dwelling in watchfulness that is at the core and heart of Quaker practice does not consist in the continual reception of messages. Rather it consists of a constant, or frequent, awareness of where the center is and the availability to the Light. Checking in over the course of the day keeps us close to the guide and oriented to that center, as well as available for orders, should they be given.

Mature Friends go through their day by listening or looking inwardly, so that all daily tasks are exposed to or passed under the light. They might watch for any sign that what they are doing, or thinking of doing, seems rightly ordered. Often there is a sense of freedom to move forward unless some barrier is encountered inwardly. It is therefore very common if one asks a seasoned Friend to do something, for that Friend to respond with words such as, "I feel free to do that," or "I feel easy to do that." Her response indicates that she does not feel uneasy at the prospect of doing it. This uneasiness or easiness, or this freedom or lack of freedom, is really a matter of knowing, or perception, as much as of sensation or emotion. One might walk down a path and see a deep hole, and feel that the best course is to skirt it; or one may come to the end of the path and decide that he cannot proceed any further because the way is simply not clear.

This characteristic experience, of moving forward until there is some inward warning, gives rise to such expressions as, "I *felt an openness in my heart* to do so and so"; *the path closed before me*; or *I felt a burden laid upon me* (or *lifted from me*). So also Friends in the ministry many times spoke of *feeling free from* a certain place. They had discharged their duty to the best of their understanding there, and were therefore free to go on to the next place they were led, or to return home.

Throughout these descriptions we have come to a set of Quaker terms that relate to the Friends experience of the corporate body, whether in business, or in worship, or in some other venue. Much of our spiritual lives is intertwined with the spiritual condition of our meetings and others individuals whom we encounter, as well as the meeting's awareness of its members' condition. The interface between the individual's awareness of the light and the relationship of that understanding to the meeting's discernment is so central to our practice as Friends that it deserves a separate chapter.

VI
Community and the Inner Life of the Meeting; the Work of Discernment

The Kingdom of Heaven did gather us and catch us all, as in a net, and his heavenly power at one time drew many hundreds to land. We came to know a place to stand in and what to wait in; and the Lord appeared daily to us, to our astonishment, amazement, and a great admiration, insomuch that we said one unto another with great joy of heart: 'What, is the Kingdom of God come to be with men?' ... And from that day forward, our hearts were knit unto the Lord and one unto another in true and fervent love, in the covenant of Life with God; and that was a strong obligation or bond upon all our spirits, which united us one unto another. We met together in the unity of the Spirit, and of the bond of peace, treading down under our feet all reasoning about religion. (Howgill, "Testimony" n. pag.)

It is characteristic of our God to bring into a community those hearing the call to become children of the Light. The prophets were sent to the children of Israel, and also foresaw a time when all nations would be invited into God's family:

In that day shall there be a highway out of Egypt unto Assyria, and the Assyrian shall come into Egypt, and the Egyptian into Assyria, and the Egyptians shall serve with the Assyrians. In that

> day shall Israel be the third with Egypt and Assyria, even a bless-
> ing in the midst of the land; whom the Lord of hosts shall bless,
> saying, Blessed be Egypt my people, and Assyria the work of my
> hands, and Israel mine inheritance. (Isaiah 19:23-25)

Our discipline has always held that to be a Quaker is to be a member of a particular meeting—a people visible in place and time. When centered in the life of the Spirit, a meeting is more than a mere collection of individuals present as a result of individual choice. Their gathering at meeting is evidence of the Spirit at work. As the beloved passage from Howgill quoted above reminds us, one of the works of the Holy Spirit is to gather individuals in a particular place and time, as at Pentecost, and offer them the blessing and challenge of peoplehood. A meeting as a body has a spiritual condition. The meeting can teach and be taught. An individual member's spiritual health and faithfulness is integrated into the body's life, and all the members depend on each other. Friends have found that Paul's account of corporate life can be realized: "… God hath tempered the body together, … that there should be no schism in the body; but that the members should have the same care one for another. And whether one member suffer, all the members suffer with it; or one member be honored, all the members rejoice with it. Now ye are the body of Christ" (1 Corinthians 12:24-27). We have also found that the dear unity can be lost, to our great sorrow. In this chapter, we explore some of the ways that Friends have talked about community life.

Relearning unity and diversity, meeting in Christ

Friends have always loved the feeling of unity that comes most powerfully in the gathered silence. In those moments, we seem to see the Friends in our meetings, and sometimes also the wider world, with different eyes. Truth is a gift that comes in this experience, because in those moments of Presence, love flows strongly, and the fear or defensiveness that keeps us from seeing ourselves and others fully is removed. Although it seems paradoxical, we can see and name both the good and the bad in ourselves, and others, with honesty and mercy. In this place, we taste the "peace that passeth understanding"—because it allows us to see without reserve, and to know that God is present in love as well as in judgment.

We can also consider differences and diversities in a freer way at such moments of transformed perception. In many instances, difference and diversity can feel threatening, no matter how often and hopefully we tell ourselves that they are gifts, and a source of strength. So they are, but only if we are in some way in touch with the life of God whose vision and love embraces the endless, unfolding diversity of our beautiful world, and the multitudes of our fellow humans. Diversity from that point of view is unsurprising and expected, and one effect of God's power is to enable us to live in diversity, and yet in a unity of spirit. "This is the true ground of love and unity, not that such a man walks and does just as I do, but because I feel the same Spirit and life in him" (Penington 1: 386, echoing Romans 14). This unity is not a matter of thinking or willing, but of *feeling* ("in the place that knows") the common life, and steadily turning towards it, even if at some cost. Fox writes:

> Because the Seed is one which is Christ and he is the Master ... all brethren, who are in the Spirit, are one. You have all one Eye, which is the Light; one fire, which consumes all which the Light discovers to be evil; and one Spirit, that baptizes all into the one body, where there is no confusion, but pureness and oneness." (Epistle 46)

Even though we are led by an infallible Spirit, stability and persistence in faithfulness are a constantly maintained condition: homeostasis in the body of Christ. Fox continues: "Therefore, all Friends mind the oneness and that which keeps you in the oneness and unity...." Fox, like any perceptive member of a people, recognizes that it is possible to wander (jump, run) out of the Light, and thus out of the oneness: we can be led into oneness by minding the Seed, but we can separate again. Although the group can be led into right action, and the Spirit can help us discover community structure consistent with its guidance, the individuals are the living stones of the unity, the factors in the structure. *We must each dwell in faithfulness, if we hope to be led faithfully as a people* (Drayton, "Unity," 23).

* * *

A living meeting

Friends have some well-loved terms to describe a *living* meeting, that is, a group which for a time dwells in the sense of the divine life, and holds those present in a stillness in which much spiritual activity takes place. Barclay describes this experience in a familiar passage from the *Apology*:

> when I came into the silent assemblies of God's people I felt a secret power among them which touched my heart, and as I gave way unto it, I found the evil weakening in me and the good raised up, and so I became thus knit and united unto them, hungering more and more after the increase of this Power and Life. (Barclay 300)

Such meetings are *covered* by the sense of God's presence and *owned* by the One who is truly conducting the worship. When the meeting is in this condition, and the words running in our heads, the individual threads of thought and concern recede, then the worshippers find themselves alert, open, tender, and communicating wordlessly. The content is a seamless blend of praise, confession, petition, thanksgiving, and a quiet, joyful acceptance of the path ahead.

In such times, Friends may be especially aware of the worshippers as a body through which a single life flows: we are *gathered*. In our profoundest prayer we can hardly separate our prayer to God from God's response to us (Romans 8), and at such times we also feel boundaries and barriers drop away between us and our companions. In this condition, we recognize with love the things that make each person a distinct creation, illuminated from within by a Light we recognize with joy and welcome. Such awareness may come at any time in a meeting, but may be particularly welcome in periods in a meeting's life when the diversity, or even disunity, has been evident and perhaps troubling. The awareness of being *gathered* comes as a powerful, yet gentle, evidence of God's bringing help, and the offer of transformation, to those who seek to walk in the Light.

Of course, just as individuals have times of more and of less centeredness, so do meetings. As one gains more experience in meetings for worship, one learns that an hour of worship can feel as though it contains different kinds of silence. It can be likened to a quiet journey down a river, with areas where the water seems widely spread across shallows, with some deeper channels. Yet the same river has other areas where the waters gather together and move gently in deep and quiet pools, or places where the water moves swiftly and with more power in a focused flood. The flood opens out again, and the water moves with less force, leaving room for backwaters and quiet eddies as it flows onward. So we find that the silence of a meeting may have different qualities at different times—restful or searching, joyful or sorrowful, focused or scattered.

Meetings have spiritual conditions

Meetings have conditions that are both chronic and temporary, interwoven with and emergent from the lives of its members. Some Friends are particularly sensitive to these conditions, and the journals of traveling ministers often comment upon the health of the meetings that they are drawn in love to visit. A Friend's "reading" of the meeting's condition may open the way to spoken ministry, or to silent striving or companionship in prayer.[28] Martha Routh put into words how she experienced this "seeing," so central to the work of a minister:

> While sitting under the renewal of baptism, I had to believe that the state of the meeting was very complicated. But it is only for thee to read, oh fellow traveler, thou who art able to do it, in a

---

28 The close attention to the condition of the meeting has often given a distinctive character to Quaker ministry. Thomas Clarkson wrote: "With respect to Quaker sermons being sometimes less connected or more confused than those of others, they would admit that this might apparently happen; and they would explain it in the following manner. Their ministers, they would say, when they sit among the congregation, are often given to feel and discern the spiritual states of individuals then present, and sometimes to believe it necessary to describe such states, and to add such advice as these may seem to require. Now these states being frequently different from each other, the description of them, in consequence, may sometimes occasion an apparent inconsistency in their discourses on such occasions. The Quakers, however consider all such discourses, or those in which states are described, as among the most efficacious and useful of those delivered." See Thomas Clarkson, *A Portraiture of Quakerism*, vol. 2 (New York: Samuel Stansbury, 1806), 252.

similar line, what it is to be so engaged, and how great the care and watchfulness which is necessary, even when under the holy anointing. The states of the people are opened like flowers in a garden, some appearing beautiful to the eye, and affording a pleasant savor; others of a contrary appearance yielding an offensive smell; others having little or no scent. To know how the culturing hand should be turned upon these, in order to help, is indeed a weighty matter; and nothing short of that adorable wisdom, which alone is profitable to direct, can accomplish it according to the divine will. (215)

Bill and Brian both have had the experience of sitting down in meeting for worship, with eyes closed for concentration, and as the meeting settles towards the center, being given a sense of those present as points of light, distinct beautiful presences. The reader may have her own way of experiencing the spirits gathered and breathing together towards God, keeping a sweet watch in the common life.

Friends have found that meetings can have negative or positive conditions.[29] These are described with a diversity of terms, such as *uncomfortable* versus *comfortable*; *light and airy* versus *weighty*; *afloat* (or *frothy*) versus *grounded (rooted, established) in the Truth*; *gathered/centered*, or *shattered*; *hard* or *tender*; *dark* or *light*; *lovely, sweet, memorable*. Spiritually sensitive visitors, such as Martha Routh, may take note of how the meeting first appears as a worship time begins; what happens during the meeting, including ministry offered; and then what the condition of the meeting appears to be as they depart. These circumstantial descriptions, however brief, suggest how carefully some Friends observe the climate of a meeting, and its weather hour by hour, or even moment by moment. Such Friends are concerned to keep themselves as centered and inwardly clear as possible, so as to avoid projecting their own conjectures and prior opinions onto the situation, thus rendering themselves unreliable instruments.

---

29 Recall in Revelation chapters 2 and 3 the letters to the seven churches, each with its abiding spirit and character, to be instructed by the Spirit.

Communication within a meeting for worship

When individuals in a meeting find themselves drawn into the Center, they may become aware that their own inward work that day has been aided by others who have gone before. Most any experienced worshipper who is moved by a concern to pray for the meeting's condition can help *settle* a meeting. Perhaps he arrives early and begins turning towards the Light, and opening into its quiet power; or she may begin upholding the meeting even while still physically traveling to the meetinghouse. Friends also sometimes find themselves upholding their community in worship even when they cannot be present physically.

Children, and former children, often find their attention drawn to some who have begun the worship early and helped the meeting to settle. There are many reminiscences from Quaker children about simply looking at the faces of some of their elders on the facing bench who seemed to be sitting in a Presence that the child did not yet know how to name. For example, Joshua Evans wrote:

> I often rode on the same horse with [my mother] to Evesham meeting ... some of those meetings were seasons of favour to me, never to be forgotten. The solid sitting of some Friends frequently reached me and touched my heart. (Evans 4)

When Joshua Evans wrote of *solid sitting*, he testified to the effectiveness of a nonverbal process that over and over has touched the lives of Friends and seekers. The content of this process is that the person observed is in a place of assurance. There is no quantifying, no claim of final answers to all questions, but merely an attitude of confident listening to a Voice from whom one has grown accustomed to receiving guidance, counsel, comfort, and reproof. Regardless of the lessons still needed, such a person has come to know the inward and dependable Teacher of whom Isaiah and Fox preached.

Perhaps you, the reader, have had the experience that, after a time of settling in meeting, you find yourself, without losing the sense of inward openness, looking around the room and cherishing the faces of those you sit with. In such a clarified moment, when your own spirit is both very calm and very alert, you are most receptive to the states and wordless testimonies of the other worshippers. You can see each one clearly, and without denying anything you might know about them, good or bad, you can see how they are beloved, how they occupy their own right place in the people of God, how your own judgments of affection or disapproval are quite beside the point. Their sitting in meeting enables your worship. At such a time, your own face shines with the sort of love we strive so hard for—though like Moses returning from Sinai, you do not notice the light you are contributing to this focal moment.

At such a time, your sitting is solid. You are settled in the Presence of the living Christ, and under the Spirit's hand. In this condition, our aspirations, not yet realized, are legitimately part of our testimony. We are wary of "seeming to be better than we are," even to ourselves. Yet when we center upon God and open to God, our potential growth is a gift from that Spirit. In Christ there is no east or west, and all times are one. So, also, the many selves we are (and wish to be, and have been) are present, and the boundaries between one version of ourselves and another grow thin. The Light can convey us towards our hopes, and can help us define our commitments and our constraints, just as it can unite the minds of people sharing the worship. It can also connect us in prayer with persons far off whose bond with us has been tenuous or unimagined.

This is the place where we are available for an inward realignment of our lives with God. Our inward order or disorder is revealed, and we can be reshaped as vessels to better contain something of the Light poured out upon us. With all aspects of our selves present, we can move more freely toward response to a concern, toward integrity, and inward to God, and outward to our brothers and sisters. From here comes ministry that arises in love and serves towards abundance of life.

In this place, the possibilities of life with God amidst our daily round are confirmed. Our inward freedom can affect the meeting, and invite others to that place, even while we know we often lose our way. We cannot let ourselves forget: the moment in worship when we feel this groundedness and confidence is as real as times of doubt or unfaithfulness. This knowledge is for our nourishment.

We can return to this place of hope and confidence; it is our Exodus moment to remember. We learn good paths to it in daily worship, divine reading, conversations, and our deeds. Every time we find a new path, it adds to our inward substance and increases the drawing power of that wordless, creating Center whom we are coming to know. This posture, made up of a balance of trial and error, confidence and crisis, blessings first-hand and otherwise, inward experience and thankfulness—all this results, on a First Day morning, in *solid sitting.*[30]

Barclay, in the same section of the *Apology* quoted above, writes with power and experience about the kinds of inward work that can occur during the meeting. His account makes clear that, while the influence of watchful spirits on those not yet settled can be unconscious, sometimes we can be aware of the individual, inward processes that are actually part of a flow of healing and guiding power shared by many or all in the place:

> sometimes, when one hath come in that hath been unwatchful, and wandering in his mind, or suddenly out of the hurry of outward business, & so not inwardly gathered with the rest, so soon as he retires himself inwardly, this Power, being in a good measure raised in the whole meeting, will suddenly lay hold upon his spirit, and wonderfully help to raise up the good in him and beget him into the sense of the same Power, to the melting and warming of his heart, even as the warmth would take hold upon a man that is cold, coming in to a stove, or as a flame will lay hold upon some little combustible matter lying near unto it. (Barclay 299)

Another example of a silent interaction that can be felt is when a meeting loses its way for while, and a faithful spirit helps to re-center the meeting by maintaining and even intensifying the focus. Many Friends have the ability to feel when a meeting has become scattered, but there is a strong inclination to feel the pain or confusion of this, and be overcome. It is a gift of the Spirit when Friends, sensing the meeting's laboring, are able to hold the meeting in prayer and help it re-center. Barclay continues in the same passage:

---

30 This passage is adapted from Brian Drayton, "On Solid Sitting," which first appeared in *Friends Journal*, March 1990.

Yea, if it fall out that several met together be straying in their minds, though outwardly silent, and so wandering from the measure of grace in themselves (which through the working of the enemy and negligence of some may fall out) if either one come in, or may be in, who is watchful, and in whom the Life is raised in a great measure, as that one keeps his place he will feel a secret travail for the rest in a sympathy with the Seed which is oppressed in the other and kept from arising by their thoughts and wanderings; and as such a faithful one waits in the Light, and keeps in this divine work, God oftentimes answers the secret travail and breathings of his own Seed through such a one, so that the rest will find themselves secretly smitten without words, and that one will be as a midwife, through the secret travail of his soul, to bring forth the Life in them, just as a little water thrown into a pump brings up the rest, whereby Life will come to be raised in all and the vain imaginations brought down, and such a one is felt by the rest to minister life unto them without words. (299-300)

The power of this divine Life can also reach a hostile or skeptical spirit. The meeting itself may have reached so solid a place of tenderness, innocence, and freedom from fear, that it can receive and help transform anger or difference. Barclay reports from his own experience:

Yea, sometimes when there is not a word in the meeting, but all are silently waiting, if one come in that is rude and wicked and in whom the power of darkness prevaileth much, perhaps with an intention to mock or do mischief, if the whole meeting be gathered into the Life, and it be raised in a good measure, it will strike terror into such an one, and he will feel himself unable to resist, but by the secret strength and virtue thereof the power of darkness in him will be chained down. (300)

Although Barclay speaks of a scoffer or enemy, the experience he describes is familiar to worshippers who are not scornful or hostile! Many of us can recall times when we have come to meeting unsettled, alienated, or at odds with ourselves and others—and the "secret power" of God's life working in and through the meeting brought relief and sometimes healing, or a path towards it. When Friends speak of *having care* of a meeting, they allude to a watchfulness that can sense the spiritual and emotional movements in a meeting, and offer patient solidity in prayer, as an anchor or point of orientation.

Staying in the life

Friends have also testified that if we live under the guidance of the Holy Spirit, we may be given to sense also when a meeting or an individual is *out of the life*. This is when someone or something is not gathered, paying attention to, or giving prime importance to, the life of God. Friends have always taken seriously the admonition to "try the spirits" and sometimes reminded each other of the proverb, "The ear trieth words as the mouth tasteth meat" (Job 34:3)—meaning that in a community where the Spirit leads us as it led the prophets before us, that Spirit will also give ability to discern. We will learn to distinguish what tastes of the Life, and what does not.

Ministers recorded many instances in which meetings they visited were not centered in the divine life. Such visitors, alert as they were to signs of a meeting's spiritual health, were able at times to feel that the meeting as a whole was sleepy and unresponsive—the members were not practicing the disciplines that enable us to wait expectantly, let go of our affairs for a while, and open simply to the Light together. In the famous "sermon of the Weeping Cross," Luke Cock ends by saying, "I thought to have a watering tonight, but ye struggle so I cannot get you together. We mun have no watering tonight, I mun leave you every yan to his own Guide" (London Yearly Meeting, §42; see Glossary for *watering*).

But the ministers noted, too, that in many meetings there was a mixture of those who were "living," or a "living remnant," as well as those who were not living faithfully. Samuel Bownas sums up what he found in Ireland in 1740:

> I found in that nation a brave, zealous, and living people in the root of true religion and discipline ... well qualified with experience in divine wisdom; but there were also some who seemed very

perfect in the form, and appeared to the outward very exact and zealous against pride and worldly customs, but, for all that, the inside was not right so that I found often very close exercise among them. (205)

Ministers took comfort from those Friends in whom God's influence was evident. Ministers who spoke in the Life also offered comfort to such people, who might be feeling isolated or needing spiritual nourishment. It is in the Life that a meeting's faithfulness and health is renewed. The Spirit's influence can spread, like a gentle radiance or a propelling wind, from the light such Friends make manifest.

It is in this life, and under the purifying power of the light, that healthy meetings undertake the business of making decisions and enacting the meeting's business. If members are practiced in attention to the Light, and have learned the taste of unity in the Spirit, they will be able to feel whether a course of action will maintain the unity or not. The intent to move towards unity with God and the community is the heart of the Quaker business process, which thus has two aims in any decision: first, to keep the meeting in love and unity with the Spirit and each other, and second, to act in outward affairs in such a way that their practice is in accord with the Spirit, and keeps the members grounded in the shared divine life. Naturally, the Quaker language reflects this view of the process. Whereas modern Friends very often assent to a course of action by saying "I approve," it once was more common to declare, "I am easy with this." Such a curious phrase fits well into Quaker spiritual understanding when we remember that the opposite of "easy" in this case would be "uneasy" or "not easy in my mind."

Individual discernment in a living community

A meeting's faithfulness depends in great measure on the faithfulness of its members. A meeting's discernment and sensitivity, its ability to preserve unity even when there is diversity of opinion, is made possible because some of its members are dwelling in the unity before the meeting even gathers for worship or business. A meeting's health is maintained if at least a core of the participants are well practiced in true waiting (which is not the same as just being silent), and the meeting is strengthened as the members, individually and together, practice living the life behind the words we have been discussing.

Our "purpose" in centering is to move into an altered state of consciousness in which we become aware of the ordering, orienting power of the Spirit. We don't worship in order to receive messages, or otherwise accomplish our own agenda, but to realign our will, understanding, and values with God's. Once we reach that place of clarity, we can in our prayer bring a need, a question, or a hope, so that it is illuminated. When we move from a period, perhaps in a First Day meeting for worship, or at some other time and setting, in which the consciousness of Christ's presence is at center stage, into the other facets of life outside of meeting, we can stay *gathered* even as we do so. In this way, the consciousness of the Holy most directly helps us see the holiness present in our daily affairs. As we maintain or refresh that awareness, dipping back into a fuller state of attention from time to time (even for a microsecond), we are also able to be aware when we are acting or speaking in a way that separates us from the Presence, or dulls it; and this is warning and invitation to re-chart our course. So it is possible to dwell in watchfulness; and from the earliest days of the movement, "In some ordinary activities no special guidance was looked for, and it was enough that Friends found in themselves no contrary balks or 'stop to their minds'" (Barbour 114).

Friends have long loved the story of Loveday Hambly (1604-1682), the Friend whose house in Cornwall, mentioned in Fox's *Journal*, became a "southern Swarthmoor."[31] She became convinced in middle life, and her inn offered hospitality and succor to traveling Friends, and those who, like her, suffered for the Truth. Her practice of "frequent retirement" in the midst of a busy life is described thus, in a memorial notice by Benjamin Coale:

It was my lot to be a household servant to her for about two years and she was more like a mother to me than a mistress. Under many

---

31 Swarthmoor Hall, near Ulverston, Cumbria, was the home of Margaret Fell, an important early leader among Friends in the north of England. Her administrative gifts made Swarthmoor an important organizing center for the new movement.

trials and sufferings she was very valiant and cheerful; she had a great family and God gave her a great measure of wisdom to order it. Her tables were plentifully spread and she took great care that all might have sufficient and that none of the good creatures which God had given her should be abused or wasted. Many times in the day as she had opportunity she retired to her closet and many times came out amongst her family in a cool and tender frame of spirit as one whose strength was inwardly renewed. (quoted in *The Friend*, Vol XVII, 165-6)

Many Friends seek to develop a habit of mindfulness, sometimes drawing on the insights of other traditions such as Buddhist or Catholic practice (perhaps not aware of the resources available within Quakerism itself!). The key is to adopt something that is simple and can be woven into one's daily life. Bill often sought and spoke of such practices, such as developing the habit of a brief "touch" of prayer when passing through a doorway. For many years, he loved to set out a little bell at the beginning of a retreat or workshop, and encourage anyone to ring it gently to signal or invite a moment of mindfulness. The moment of silent grace before meals, or just before setting out on a journey, is another way to take some frequent, ordinary occurrence, and use such brief moments of explicit prayerful contact to keep ourselves woven into the fabric of a steady, unseen fabric of awareness.

It is sometimes very encouraging when we have the opportunity to hear how other people maintain this daily, simple consciousness. Brian once visited a meeting when traveling under a concern to encourage just such conversations. At an evening gathering, after a potluck and a period of worship, he asked, "Do you have some daily practice of 'retirement'? At least occasionally? Can you describe it?" What followed was a very precious time, as a group of Friends, perhaps already opened in the worship that evening, shared freely with each other. Everyone present spoke about whether they had a practice or not, and what form it took. Most of them did not feel that they completely had realized their ideal. Some felt free to say that they had not yet been able to really develop a practice. In hearing the testimony of other Friends at that time, the group felt that whatever faithfulness each had come to was something to be grateful for, and something to use as a starting place for a fuller practice; and everyone heard many different ways to keep the daily watch.

Leadings

Learning how to explore and discern whether leadings, promptings, or nudgings are from God is important, but Friends have never assumed that at the highest pitch of spiritual attainment everything turns into a leading whose origins must be discerned. After all, the first goal of inward work is to come before God's presence, whether in singing or contrition or some moment of need, waiting until we are worshipping in spirit and in truth:

> Stand still in that which is pure, after you see yourselves, and then Mercy comes in. After you see your thoughts and temptations, do not think but submit. Then the Power comes. Stand still in the Light and submit to it, and the other will be hushed and gone. Then contentment comes. When temptations and troubles appear, sink down into that which is pure, and all will be hushed and fly away. Your strength is to stand still ... (Fox, Epistle 10)

Whether we feel fully immersed in the living stream of divine life, or whether we are just walking in our daily paths, we may feel something that we have not noticed before. A name, an event, a location, or a task may become present to us. Then we begin the process of discernment, and if we have traveled a little in the inward landscape, we can see that we want to know, which is: "Does this thing I am shown have life?" At first, all we may know is that something is coming back again and again, but we may not see any further. At some point, we might share the simple prompting with another Friend. We should keep close to the opening, being careful to keep separate the sense of leading (in which the life can be felt) and our own contributions of thought and imagination, although these may furnish important material with which to work if the hints and nudges grow into a concern. The voyage of the Woodhouse, another famous story from the early days of the Quaker movement, as told by Robert Fowler, illustrates the early stages of a concern:

This vessel was appointed for this service from the beginning, as I have often had it manifested unto me, that it was said within me several times:— "Thou hast her not for nothing"; and also New England presented before me. And also, when she was finished and freighted and made to sea, contrary to my will [the vessel] was brought to London, where, speaking touching this matter to Gerrard Roberts and others, they confirmed the matter in behalf of the Lord, that it must be so. Yet, entering into reasoning and letting in temptations and hardships, and the loss of my life, wife and children with the enjoyment of all earthly things, it brought me as low as the grave and laid me as one dead as to the things of God. But by His instrument George Fox was I refreshed and raised up again...[and] by the strength of God I was made willing to do His will. (Fowler, in Bowden 63-6)

If the inward prompting continues, we find ourselves seeking further clearness or clarity. *Clearness, clear,* and *clarity* constitute another important, and familiar, Quaker word family; closely related are *free* and *freedom.* Friends speak of being *clear*—or *not clear* — to proceed with a plan, to travel, to depart from a place; often in similar cases, Friends may use *free*: "I was not yet free from this place"; "I found freedom to speak to him." Nowadays we often say that someone has been *found clear* after a "clearness process" or by a "clearness committee" by the meeting. Friends in the past often also said, "I was liberated by my brethren," and this term recalls the beloved, profound idea of "Gospel liberty," the freedom of the Gospel of love, preached and lived by Jesus, and taught so passionately by Paul, who reminds us that "the love of Christ constrains us" (2 Corinthians 5:14).[32] This constraint is not a restraint, but a channeling of our minds and actions, and a way-making by divine love.

Sometimes, perhaps often, we find that "leadings"—a sense that we are being required to do something—are accompanied by "openings," fresh insight into some aspect of Truth. From the early days of the Quaker movement, these have been seen as two different operations of the Holy Spirit:

32 For a beautiful meditation on this passage, see Geoffrey Nuttall, "Love's Constraints," in *Early Quaker studies and the divine presence* (Weston Rhyn, Wales: Quinta Press, 2003), 265-272.

Friends have always needed to distinguish between "Openings" teaching them timeless truths, and "Call" experiences of individual guidance for specific tasks and decisions. Even the latter, however, were tested by early Friends against the discerning of other Friends, to guard against self-deception. For example, Thomas Stubbs, though his own work kept him in Northampton, spoke of feeling the call that had taken Edward Burrough and Francis Howgill to Ireland. At the same time he wrote to William Dewsbury, in prison for his faith, that he felt united to him in the will of the Lord. (Barbour, "Five tests" and see Barbour 1991)

We should remember this distinction as we undertake discernment about some inward motion. We may come to understand something, without it entailing—at the moment of realization — any specific action, though such an opening, because it changes the way we understand the world, will shape future deeds and thoughts. But the excitement of "Aha!" is not in itself a commission. When George Fox had his great openings, he said that, with the new vision into the heart of things, he "was at a stand in my mind whether to practice physic for the good of mankind, seeing the nature and virtues of the creatures were so opened to me by the Lord" (Fox, Journal, 27). But his actual commission was otherwise.

The prophets were aware of the dangers that come from "running when you were not sent." A leading of service under the Spirit's guidance involves the prepared messenger, the formation of the message, and the preparation of the recipient. Mistaking one's mission can create discouragement or hardness in the receiver, or the messenger, or both:

I have not sent these prophets, yet they ran: I have not spoken to them, yet they prophesied. But if they had stood in my counsel, and had caused my people to hear my words, then they should have turned them from their evil way, and from the evil of their doings. (Jeremiah 23:21-22)

Quakers learned this lesson not only from the Scriptures, but also from their own experience. They also learned that even a great and faithful prophet like Moses can act in his own power and result important spiritual consequences. In Numbers 20, when the children of Israel cry out for water in the wilderness of Zin, Moses asks God for guidance. Moses is told to gather the people and speak to a rock to make the water flow; but instead he upbraids the people for their discontent and strikes the rock with his staff, as he did before. The water comes forth, but Moses is denied entry into the Promised Land for his reliance, we may say, on his own judgment or past achievement, instead of relying on the command given for the people at this moment. Friends digested the implications of this story, found it confirmed in their own lives, and often reminded each other of it.

Hence we must take care in discerning whether a true leading is given us, for whom it is meant, and when it is to be enacted. The journals of Friends report many instances in which they wait, and wait again. Another favorite Biblical allusion in this connection was "to try the fleece both wet and dry," referring to the time when Gideon, uncertain what God was commanding him to do, asks God to give him a sign—twice—before he presumed to go to Israel claiming a divine commission (Judges 6).

As we seek how to best respond to the leading, and wait for clarity, the way may open or may close. This may be because of an inward change, or some outward circumstance. This is an important lesson of stewardship to bear in mind—when a leading seems to come, and to come with life, we are likely going to start shaping our expectations for how to carry it out, and sometimes to imagine the good that will come when we have done it. While this is natural, Friends have found over the years that a discipline of faithfulness frees us from deep attachment to the outcomes of our leadings, and allowing ourselves to be so attached can itself make us less sensitive to guidance, and less willing to serve again. Yet if we can bear in mind that it is the Seed of Christ, embodied in God's children, that we wish to serve, we can learn to trust the Seed to reach to its own, in its time.

We should also be willing to consider without fear whether a leading is being withdrawn. This may happen for reasons that have little or nothing to do with us. It need not mean failure, but just that we have been as faithful as required. In 1823, Joseph Hoag felt drawn to pay a visit to Friends throughout several yearly meetings. Because, he wrote, he had been active in upholding meeting discipline, he had made some enemies, who were not comfortable in supporting his leading: "… in so doing, I had offended so many, that they would not let me go. My Master returned the answer, 'Do what I bid thee, and if I do not make way for thee, thou shalt be clear'" (Hoag 249).

Another famous example comes from John Woolman's journal (153-159), when he is sure that he is called to undertake a journey to the West Indies, seeks and obtains clearness from his meeting, and even got to the port ready to leave, but then felt the concern taken from him.

In a narrative rich with many of the inward language terms, another example illustrates how the individual and the meeting can explore a leading:

> The Meeting of Ministers and Elders considered the Minute respect-ing Thomas Shillitoe's visit to Holland, Germany, and France This sitting was such a season of deep exercising travel, as divers Friends expressed they had scarse remembered. The Meeting seemd to be baptized together as into a cloud, where, for a time, no light appeared to shine so as to afford sufficient evidence that it would be best to proceed towards liberating [him]. Divers Friends expressed their doubts ... Thomas informed the Meeting how he continued to feel respecting the subject. He said that since the preceding meeting, he had endeavored to feel whether the trial of his faith in communicating the concern ... would not have been accepted as the ram for the sacrifice; but in his indeavoring to feel after the will of his Heavenly Father, he could not witness his mind to be released, without still casting his burthen upon the Meeting for it to dispose of him ... he would not take one step therein without the unity of his Friends. It seemed to me like deep calling under deep ... in time the cloud gradually appeared to disperce, till at length ... the Clerk could form a minute recording that the Meeting sweetly united in liberating our beloved Friend. (*Pen Pictures* 86)

Formation in community life

In considering discernment, we come back to terms that we have seen before: to *wait*, to *living in the Cross*, to the *Cross of Joy* and *going to the place that knows*. These words represent a way of living, a kind of awareness and attitude of preparation, which is both a gift of the spirit, and a result of formation and practice. Formation is a community experience, and it is in community we first can test what seems to be inward growth by the reality of action and interaction. It is all too possible for us to talk without life, as Bownas reported in the passage quoted above, to seem perfect on the outside, but not be right inside. We can give too much sway to "feelings" which may only be self-expressions, or expressions of our culture (the meeting culture or the wider culture). The acerbic James Jenkins reported, from the late 1700s:

> In those days, almost every Friend was a <u>feeler</u>; no act of scarcely any importance [was undertaken] without first [being] <u>felt</u> to be right, but which however the event did not always confirm, and I am afraid that the hackneyed profession of feeling was often an unnecessary, if not an ostentatious display of our common belief in divine revelation. (37)

Although our Guide is true, we are not always correct or complete in our understanding, and we must learn to accept with humility, and sometimes humor, that we can be wrong in our discernment. Our watchfulness and work in the end is not to focus on self, but on the divine life, at work and in part discernible in ourselves, or our meeting, or in any of God's children.

The meeting for worship is one place to learn this kind of alertness to the inward motion, and its appropriate clothing in outward action. For example, it sometimes happens that a watchful Friend, feeling the condition of the meeting gathered in worship, can understand that *someone else* is summoned to speak, and even something of the content of the message that is rising. Many can describe times when they felt a message rise, only to have it spoken by another, or spoken piecemeal by many voices attuned to the exercise of the meeting. Indeed, someone who often speaks in meeting may do well, when a hint comes that a message may be called for, to wait and seek in prayer whether the message truly discerned is better given by another who is feeling the call. Then the work is to support that other Friend in her faithfulness.

It sometimes happens, too, that in such a dialogue in the silence of the meeting, a Friend is given to know when someone was called for the meeting's help, but shrank from the task. Love and forthrightness then prompt an act of nurturing comment:

> ... we were at Mamaroneck meeting. Here, finding my mind led into different subjects, I was thoughtful to close in good season; but after sitting down, I did not feel that clear quiet, which I commonly feel when I time it right; but being unwilling to rise again, or kneel [to offer vocal prayer] —for my mind was arrested with both—I sat until it wore off, and then broke the meeting. After I got out, an Elder came and took me by the hand, and said, "Joseph, thou has been preaching to others to be faithful to their gifts; hast thou been faithful to thine? I confess I did not expect the meeting to end so," and turned away. Though I did not expect to be found out in that way, I was glad to meet with such honesty from the Friend. (Hoag 153)

But the meeting for business, and the other shared activities of the community life, are a crucial testing ground for the truths (of understanding or of calling) that we believe we have found in inwardness in worship. Worshipping in spirit *and* in truth is a challenge for us! As the Gospels show, even at a time when Christ was present in the flesh, disciples could discover that their good intentions and beliefs could evaporate under the test of action.

> The true knowledge of the way, with the walking in the way, is reserved for God's child, -- for God's traveller. Therefore keep in the regeneration, keep in the birth: be no more than God hath made thee. Give over thine own willing; give over thine own running; give over thine own desiring to know or to be any thing, and sink down to the seed which God sows in the heart, and let that grow in thee, and be in thee, and breathe in thee, and act in thee. (Penington 2: 205)

And so in worship, and in the community life that grows out of it, we are formed, so that we become more hospitable and responsive to Christ's Spirit. We can take encouragement from our own (and others') experiences of growth in the ability to feel and act from the prophetic stream of divine life, and in returning to it with fresh expectation, find ourselves reliably renewed, strengthened, and touched by joy.

VII

The Inward Landscape: Walking With the Ministers

The tension between inward discovery and outward faithfulness, individual inspiration and community discernment—these fundamentals of Quaker spirituality, *realized* spirituality—are portrayed searchingly and humbly in the Quaker journals. The journals left by generations of ministering Friends are perhaps the best place to encounter the full range of the Quaker language for the inward landscape. As they sought to follow their calling faithfully, ministers had to be increasingly attentive and skilled at noticing and understanding the events and processes of the inward life, both in themselves and in those they were called to serve. Indeed, the life of concern is a life on a razor's edge, as Bill Taber once wrote (Taber 1996). It is the edge between waiting and action, between the promptings of self and of the divine life moving through human personality. It is a boundary along which many Friends (and others) find themselves, the boundary along which God's will breaks into history.

If we read these accounts "Quaker style," meditatively, and informed by our experience of the Spirit that guided the ministers and also guides us, we come into a place where we can feel something of their life and the meaning of their language. As we do this, we can discover things about Quaker spiritual practice, and the role of vocal ministry, that can offer resources to the life of our meetings, and to all Friends, whether they are called to ministry or not. We rarely have such detailed reports from across someone's spiritual lifespan from "non-ministers," or Friends whose callings and areas of spiritual growth have not been organized by a call to vocal ministry. Perhaps you, reader, might find a concern to help address this deficiency!

The Root and Motive of Ministry

What is the purpose of vocal ministry in worship and in the life of the meeting? Let us start by considering the vantage point from which the ministers examined their own inward life, and the lives of their communities. Friends have often emphasized that the aim of all religious exercise was to bring the individual to God's presence as fully as the person's measure of light permitted:

> Those who are brought to a pure still waiting upon God in the spirit, are come nearer to the Lord than words are; for God is a spirit, and in the spirit is he worshiped. . . . In such a meeting there will be an unwillingness to part asunder, being ready to say in yourselves, it is good to be here; and this is the end of all words and writings—to bring people to the eternal living Word. (Alexander Parker, in A. R. Barclay [33]365-366)

Many ministering Friends warned of the human tendency to look forward, not to the moment of centering in the Presence of God, but rather to hope, "with itching ears" (2 Timothy 4:3) to hear some human exhortation, guidance, or emotional appeal.

The purpose of ministry is "to bring people to Christ and leave them there." There have been times and places in Quakerism when the privilege of silent worship has been so highly emphasized that silence has become the ideal ("The only thing that the ministry requires is universal suppression," said one Friend at a nineteenth century session of London Yearly Meeting), and there are Friends today to whom this ideal is attractive. But traditionally, Friends have taken both the warrant of Scripture and their own experience as evidence that vocal ministry, under the right circumstances, plays a valuable part in the religious life of the meeting. It

---

33 Except where indicated, such as here, all references to Barclay refer to Robert Barclay.

can awaken the sleeper, disconcert the complacent, refresh the spiritually weary, instruct or point out the path to spiritual growth, and comfort those who are in mourning or overcome by spiritual poverty.

> Our safest eloquence is our silence. It behoveth our words to be wary and few. Let all earth keep silence before him. Friends understand this well. But it is also joy to make mention of his name. How beautiful are the feet of him that bringeth good tidings, that publisheth peace; thy watchmen lift up their voice, they sing for joy. Early Friends rejoiced to be publishers of truth: to be great in declaration. (Nuttall 19)

The fundamental root and motive for the ministry as Friends have understood it is a motion of love, a concern for the spiritual flourishing of others, and a delight in the experience of God's presence.

> From an inward purifying and steadfast abiding under it, springs a lively operative desire for the good of others. All faithful people are not called to the public ministry, but whoever are, are called to minister of that which they have tasted and handled spiritually. The outward modes of worship are various, but wherever men are true ministers of Jesus Christ, it is from the operation of his spirit upon their hearts, first purifying them, and thus giving them a feeling sense of the conditions of others. (Woolman 31)

> Thou deep wader for the good of souls, this is wrote principally for thy sake, that thou mayest see others have gone the same way before thee, and be encouraged so as not to sink under thy burden. I found in the Lord's time (as thou wilt, if thou patiently holds on thy way) that tribulation worketh patience, and patience experience, and experience hope. (Griffith 118)

Anyone may offer the ministry that is needed at a particular moment: God is free to choose anyone as a messenger. But Friends have acknowledged that for some, vocal ministry is a primary calling (at least for some period of time).

If it be understood of a liberty to speak or prophesy by the Spirit, I say all may do that, when moved thereunto... but we do believe and affirm that some are more particularly called to the work of the ministry and therefore are fitted of the Lord for that purpose, whose work is more constantly and particularly to instruct, exhort, admonish, oversee, and watch over their brethren; and that as there is something more incumbent upon them in that respect than upon every common believer. (Barclay 274)

Under preparation for service

Robert Barclay, writing so close to the beginnings of Quakerism, describes matters that any modern Friend can attest to. God may call anyone to the service of the meeting, which is why we are all enjoined to come "with hearts and minds prepared" to public worship. Yet as spiritual gifts are not distributed by our Leader identically to all, some find themselves called more frequently over time to speak (or as Friends often said, "appear") in vocal ministry. The experience of any sustained commitment brings with it a change of awareness appropriate to the right engagement in the work. The minister who is called to this service over many years must get better and better at discerning when she is to speak, what she is to speak, and when to be silent. For this, the minister must be prepared (fitted), learning to understand his (her) own spiritual condition, and learn to feel the condition of those with whom (s)he interacts, being continually open to guidance and spiritual connection with others in the Truth.

The preparation includes a growth in dedication to the work, and in the consistency of minister's life and acts with the Spirit of Christ — so that he provides evidence of the truthfulness of his message. Barclay puts the Quaker position clearly: a minister of the Gospel is prepared by spiritual experience, under God's tutelage. With this essential qualification, any skills or other gifts the individual may have can be consecrated for use in the service:

we make not human learning necessary, yet we are far from excluding true learning, to wit, that learning which proceedeth from the inward teachings and instructions of the Spirit, whereby the soul learneth the secret ways of the Lord, becomes acquainted with many inward travels and exercises of the mind, and learneth by a living experience how to overcome evil and the temptations of it by following the Lord and walking in his light, and waiting daily for wisdom and knowledge immediately from the revelation thereof, and so layeth up these heavenly and divine lessons in the good treasure of the heart as honest Mary did the sayings which she heard and things which she observed; and also out of this treasure of the soul, as the good scribe, brings forth things new and old, according as the same Spirit moves and gives a true liberty, and as need is for the Lord's glory, whose the soul is, and for whom, and with an eye to whose glory, she which is the temple of God learneth to do all things. This is that good learning which we think necessary to a true minister. (Barclay 260)

In the morning of Quakerism, Friends brought some strife upon themselves by asserting that a minister cannot serve if he or she has not experienced the transforming power of Christ's inward work, and therefore some degree of sanctification, as Barclay alluded to. While Friends often report that they became aware that they were "under preparation" for service in the ministry, they often struggled to deny the calling. It was in part because when one "stood as a trumpet" to declare the Gospel, the very act implied that one took on a burden, and made the claim of progress towards holiness. They knew that their words would be accepted for the power or life that might be in them, but also that the consistency of their lives would come under some scrutiny.

This is one area in which modern Friends often seem to differ from Friends in the past. In some cases, it seems that a Friend begins ministering acceptably before really becoming "concerned," and we rarely visit a Friend to suggest that his or her behavior is not in line with words spoken in meeting. Rather, it is as though such Friends, as they reflect on their experience in meeting, begin to question themselves on this point, and are drawn to make profession and possession line up. Then, drawn (perhaps to their own surprise) into the "inward work of Christ," they learn to "live in the Cross," be more self-aware, and learn by grace to grow in freedom from the demands and fears of ego, and other temptations that can beset a public Friend.

Growth in Love

The essence of the change within a Friend called to ministry, however, is a growth in love. Friends often used to say that the "drawings of Gospel love" pulled them into some service, such as a visit to distant lands, or the families in a meeting. Elizabeth Hudson wrote of a time during her travels when she was seized with this love:

> Refreshed ourselves at an inn which happens to be situated oppo-site the market and being their market day, a very numerous con-course of people there was, which I stood sometime beholding and made some serious observation upon, each one assiduously pursu-ing that branch of business that belongs to them. I felt my soul filled with concern for their immortal parts with such a degree of gospel love which wishes health and salvation to all men, which led me to breathe to God for them, even to wrestle in spirit with great fervor. I thought I felt for some time the weight of their sins and did not know but that I must go out into the street [to speak to them], which filled me with an awful dread, [but] after weigh-ing the concern [found] that no particular message offering, [and] found freedom to waive so doing. (149)

Later, this same love arose as she visited a little meeting, and she was drawn into words for the help of these Friends:

> The next day had a comfortable meeting with a few friends in those parts. I found my spirit sweetly seasoned with a larger degree of divine love than common, which greatly enlarged my heart towards them. (Hudson 247)

Bill spoke warmly of standing in some empty old meetinghouse, grip-ping the handrail in the ministers' gallery, and feeling the tide of divine caring that had flowed through others in that spot. In similar vein, Brian has often testified how, when the meeting seems to have been gathered into God's awesome and tender presence, it is a joy and a spiritual discipline to look in turn at each face, to be challenged, humbled, and kindled by the beauty that can be seen there, "in that which is eternal."

Bill sometimes spoke of "the minister's belly," a distinctive contribution of his own to the language of the inward landscape. This phrase had its roots in Bill's memory as a youth, of being embraced by Carl Patterson, a beloved, portly minister, whose solid bulk somehow reinforced his warm expression of love and concern. For Bill, "the minister's belly" expressed the sense of whole-hearted, benevolent caring that lies at the bottom of much Gospel ministry, and has the power to reach over boundaries, draw out gifts, encourage reconciliation, and overcome fear.

We must keep this love in mind, especially as we turn to other words that ministers used to describe their service. When someone like Catherine Stephens or Job Scott wrote that on a particular occasion, they found themselves "deeply exercised" (see the Glossary) or "wading deeply" as they felt the condition of a meeting, we think first of their sense of grief at the alienation from God that they felt among the Friends before them. When Samuel Bownas or Elias Hicks spoke of seeing a "wide field of doctrine" opening up as they sat, "keeping their eye" on an embryonic message rising up in them, we may find it easy to focus on the intellectual work that was involved in shaping such a message—but if they were speaking in the Life, then the love was palpable as well. Walt Whitman conveys this, in his reminiscences of Hicks's preaching heard in his boyhood:

A pleading, tender, nearly agonizing conviction, and magnetic stream of natural eloquence, before which all minds and natures, all emotions, high or low, gentle or simple, yielded entirely without exception, was its cause, method, and effect. Many, very many were in tears. (Whitman, "Notes (such as they are) Founded on Elias Hicks")

There was, however, another nuance to Bill's phrase, "the minister's belly." It could connote the inward spaciousness that comes when the minister is relying on God's strength and not his own, so that time and energy also expand to meet the needs of the moment; it comes of dwelling more and more in love. Once in an opportunity with Brian, Bill recalled Brian's description of the salt marshes he loved in his youth in Maine. Bill said, opening his arms outward, "You need to let your inward dimensions expand, so that you are carrying the space of those marshlands stretching along the rivers, the sense of inward freedom, so you can embrace others in spirit, the feeling I like to call 'the minister's belly.' You can feel it *here!*" he said, patting his own midriff.

Feeling into Faithfulness

Friends in all generations have tried to describe times when they were led to speak. They spoke of feeling "enlarged," or feeling "an enlargement of the heart," so that there was a fresh spring of life rising. This might have been preceded by a long period of exercise, as Friends were baptized into the condition of the meeting. At some point in their worship, some subject might present itself, which they would continue to focus on in meditation. As Friends accepted their calling on that occasion to speak to the meeting, they might sit long, waiting for the message to come into their grasp, and then stand and deliver what had been, as Lewis Benson put it, "given in the matrix of prayer" (49).

At other times, however, merely a phrase or line of Scripture might be given with clarity to the Friend, and yet the command to stand comes before any message forms. This is surely an intimidating experience, and yet there comes a moment in which one's natural reluctance and worries about performing well fall away. The most important thing is that one feels accompanied by the Spirit, and united with the other worshippers, so that the silence is not broken, but expressed and deepened by the words that emerge, often much to the minister's surprise.

If the meeting was not well settled, and the minister was intensely aware that something was amiss, he or she might undergo "deep wading" in the labor to speak truthfully and fully as led to the condition of the meeting. In Isaiah, we hear people who are in denial about their alienation from God cry out to the prophets, "Speak to us of smooth things!" A faithful messenger might have to speak of something very uncomfortable to the meeting, and the minister may experience "close work" in speaking home such truths into a possibly unreceptive community. If the gift were given to someone to "plow the spiritual ground," or "thresh" so that the wheat (the good seed) were to be separated from the chaff (the factors that make for complacency or spiritual coldness), hearts might be made more receptive (tender) to the word of invitation or warning.

I can truly say that my mind has been more and more concerned for the working down everything which would get up and get above the good seed. I think we are never safe unless we feel the plow of God's power and the hammer thereof so operating in us as to break us into tenderness (Morris 64)

If the messenger was faithful, he or she might record that there was "a favored time," or an "open time" in which the minister "fully cleared my mind," and thus was free of any further obligation. Sometimes, while one felt fully commissioned to speak, the work of "rightly dividing the word of truth" was burdensome, physically and intellectually as well as emotionally and spiritually. On one occasion, Martha Routh described "laboring in the Gospel," rather than preaching it in joy. She is not alone among the ministers in noting that sometimes the sense of responsibility for the spiritual life of those with whom she worshiped did not translate easily into words. Finding the way to the heart of the message, and then crafting words with which to deliver it, can involve intense focus and effort.

The reward for the minister would be peace and a solemn joy, and this also was evidence that he had been faithful in measure. Woolman writes:

… to be faithful to the Lord and to be content with his will concerning me is a most necessary and useful lesson for me to be learning, looking less at the effects of my labor than at the pure motion and reality of the concern as it arises from heavenly love. In the Lord Jehovah is everlasting strength and as the mind by a humble resignation is united to him and we utter words from an inward knowledge that they arise from the heavenly spring, and though our way may be difficult and require close attention to keep in it, and though the manner in which we may be led may tend to our own abasement, yet if we continue in patience and meekness, heavenly peace is the reward of our labors. (72)

Bill loved to recount a story of Zebedee Haines, a minister in Philadelphia Yearly Meeting, who ministered powerfully in a meeting for worship, and yet at the post-meeting potluck was lively, even jolly. An elder spoke to him privately, questioning how he could be so lightsome after such a solemn engagement. Haines replied, "My master gave me a commission, and I have carried it out to the best of my ability. Now he says I may play."

Sometimes, a minister might feel the way closed, or "shut up," and this often was taken to indicate something about the receptivity or spiritual health of the meeting. Or, as often reported from Fox's time, the minister might (no matter how strong the expectations were that he or she would speak) feel that their "portion was silence," also an important witness.

The experiences of being led or restrained in ministry intensify when the minister finds herself in an "opportunity," a spontaneous or semi-spontaneous time of worship with an individual or a small group, such as in a family. In these times, the minister might find himself drawn especially to prayer, or "speaking to conditions, " that is, delivering a message specifically to an individual. When this happens, and if it is rightly led, the experience is humbling and powerful for all concerned. Some Friends have had a particular gift or calling for this kind of intimate service. As we can testify, it is demanding as well as rewarding, and one must resist the impulse to speak just because one convened the opportunity. Brian remembers vividly times that were truly favored, but also some when he outran his guide, which is an extremely painful experience, because one feels that one has acted against the honor of Truth, and the integrity of Friends' understanding of ministry. As John William Graham said in reporting an opportunity in which the visiting minister spoke without a true leading, "The gift cannot be had by pretense" (Graham, *Psychical experiences* 34).

Friends often encouraged faithfulness and accountability in the ministry by ensuring that traveling ministers were accompanied: it is now well known that Friends tended to travel in pairs or small groups, when under a concern, following New Testament practice. Sometimes this was with an elder, a Friend who has gifts of discernment and encouragement, but who rarely is called to offer vocal ministry. Very often, too, ministers would travel together, and support and watch over each other in conversation and prayer. Such collaborations could be intense and fruitful. Friends accomplished much work, overcame challenges, and learned from experiences. Some of these partnerships lasted for many years.

It was not always the case that a Friend traveled in company. Yet guidance and oversight continued, first by the Spirit guiding the attentive servant inwardly, and also by the worshiping group itself. Long ago, Friends wrote, "It is a living ministry [that] begets a living people"[34] (Brayshaw, *The Quakers* 247), but we are also reminded, "The meeting affects the ministry quite as truly as the ministry affects the meeting" (London Yearly Meeting, §282). A healthy meeting includes people who know how to be there, who are concerned to "settle" the meeting and create an attentive, inviting space of worship, which makes it easier for others to come to the Center in their turn. Such Friends who have the gift of presence provide an important vessel for the subsequent worship, including any outward exercises of prayer or speaking. These Friends also can directly support any Friend in whom a message is rising, as he or she works towards faithful service.

We cannot leave the topic of ministry and the inward landscape without reminding ourselves, as we often should, of the powerful ministry that can be exercised in the silence itself. The journals often speak of times when ministers felt themselves "resigned," "stripped," or "empty," and very aware of the insufficiency of their own strength and talents, so that they were in a condition of entire dependence on God. Although this can be a moment of anxiety or even anguish, one can also come to welcome this sense of being stripped, recognizing it as a time of availability and integrity. Martha Routh's journal records:

> … on second day we crossed the river, and attended a meeting at Kittery 7 miles distant, which seemed for a time a low stripping season, yet not void of secret instruction to myself, and, through attention to the leadings of it, the meeting closed much more to my relief than that on the day before. (81)

Sometimes this was preparation for faithful service, as many can attest. Sometimes it marked a time when the ministers were so completely free and available that they could remain silent. Friends frequently felt that these were times of retraining, or recalibration, whose purpose was to prepare the minister more fully for some service in the future.

Both of us, Bill and Brian, can attest that times of (long) silence may be

---

34 "It is a living ministry that begets a living people; and by a living ministry at first we were reached and turned to the Truth. It is a living ministry that will still be acceptable to the Church and serviceable to its members." Testimony concerning John Banks by Somerset Quarterly Meeting, 1711.

another way for Christ to work in and through his people, even those with gifts of ministry. In such periods, one can feel no freedom to speak, but rather to contribute to the meeting's life by an active, inward participation. It may take the form of dwelling in heightened attentiveness to the Light at work in the personalities of the meeting, perhaps for the encouragement of specific gifts or callings that are taking shape in the body. Or it may be that the person who has become comfortable with the once-daunting work of vocal ministry is led into receiving messages, and then praying them silently into the meeting.

* * *

The inward landscape journey and our service in love

This chapter has drawn on stories from the experiences of Friends ministers across the centuries. We should stress that much of their experience is relevant to anyone acting on a concern, whether in vocal ministry or any other kind of service in which "love is the first motion."

As worshipers and as Children of the Light seeking to walk in that Light, the core of our witness lies in living and acting out of an awareness of God and of the divine love that is God's life, which increasingly can be ours. The Light of Christ is always present, guiding, healing, and empowering us in our measure, and flowing as a stream of life that binds us all into one body, and makes us ever more aware of the Light in which we are united. As we journey into this awesome, surprising, and joyous awareness, we cross much inward terrain, sometimes in lots of company, and sometimes quite alone. Our explorations today can be greatly enriched and nourished by the Quaker language for the inward landscape, and the travelogues and reports of Friends in other centuries, who, in God's presence, are also our contemporaries and companions along the way.

VIII
Exploring the Inward Landscape:
Some Descriptive Terms

To the reader: These terms are not intended as a complete reference list, or historical exposition, but rather as an aid to your own exploration of the inward landscape, using these terms as starting points. You are encouraged, therefore, when coming to any entry, to stop and hold the word, examining what it may suggest to you. After pausing to explore what arises in you, then go on and read the discussion. There may be material in our prose that encourages further reflection. Then spend time with the quotations provided, listening to those voices of our sisters and brothers from years past, who tried to walk the path you are taking yourself.

Take note of how often one term may occur in an entry used to illustrate a different one, and how many terms in this glossary also make some appearance in the main text. The Language for the Inward Landscape is a tapestry, with its ideas and images linked to and harmonized with each other.

Baptism, being dipped

Friends traditionally have used the word *baptism* or the phrase *being dipped.* In the primary sense, it conveys the experience of entering into a new kind or quality of life, consonant with John the Baptist's declaration (Matthew 2:11) that the one who would follow him would baptize with the Holy Spirit and with fire. Fox writes of this baptism:

> My friends ... who do witness the high calling in Christ Jesus (Phil. 3:14)... and are become new creatures...in the Light and Life wait, that with it your minds may be directed, guided and joined together with that which is immortal and undefiled, in one Spirit up to the immortal God. And with the Spirit...witness the one baptism into one body and you all in the light may see the one faith, which Christ is the author and finisher of. Then you may all see the end of your faith, the salvation of your souls with that which gives you victory over the world. (Fox, Epistle 124)

In a common secondary sense, *baptism* connotes a journey of spirit into deep and vivid sympathy with the condition of a meeting or individual. One might even describe oneself as being "baptized with the dead," that is, having a clear sense of the spiritual unhealth of a meeting or of some individuals. Such sensitivity often comes as a result of a renewed clarification in the Spirit, an exercise in which a person moves past some barrier to be freshly opened in compassion and insight to the condition of others. If you come to realize that you have been brought by the presence and power of the Spirit into this sympathy with another, it may lead you to more purposeful or directed prayer, because you may become more alert to issues about which the sympathizing Friend is exercised.

> [T]o visit the immortal life, where it lies, requires great abstractedness of mind ... Oh! sometimes when in this situation, how clearly has the state of meetings and individuals been opened, to my mind, as plain as ever I saw the face of another with my natural eyes! (Grubb 39)

Finally, *baptism* may refer to any powerful and meaningful spiritual experience, immersive in its feeling. For example, Samuel Bownas writes of a time of trial when his service in ministry seemed blocked up:

> ... the poverty of my spirit was so exceedingly great and bitter that I could scarcely bear it, but cried out loud, which so surprised my companion that he, being on foot, he feared it would be too hard for me, for I complained that I was deceived or mistaken; because,

while I was in my master's work, I rarely by day or night was without some degree of Divine virtue upon my mind, but now I could feel nothing but the bitterness of death and darkness; all comfort was hid from me for a time, and I was baptized into death indeed. As we went along, I said to Isaac with a vehemence of spirit: "Oh! that I was in my master's work again, and favored with my former enjoyments of Divine life, how acceptable it would be! (5)

Breathe
breathe towards God (prayer)

Breathe connotes a gentle, humble prayer, perhaps hardly formed into words, bearing a concern or deep longing. The usage is reminiscent of Lamentations 3:55-6: "I called upon thy name, O Lord, out of the low dungeon. Thou hast heard my voice; hide not thine ear at my breathing."

that whereby ye received the knowledge was the light within; the eye that God secretly opened in your spirits. This was the way ye then came by it, though ye perhaps might feel the thing, but not know how ye came by it, even as a babe may see truly, but doth not understand its own eye, or know how it sees. While this eye was kept open in you, your knowledge was true in its measure, and serviceable to you, and did draw you nearer to God, making you truly tender, meek, sweet, humble, patient, loving, gentle, and of precious breathings towards God, and after righteousness. Oh! how lovely were you to God in this state! (Penington 1: 223)

I felt very feeble both in body and mind. The latter became a little helped through the impression of a belief raised therein, that many brethren and sisters, from whom we were separated in body, had been caring for us, and breathing on our behalf, both in public and private, to the great Preserver of Men. (Routh 60)

But another connotation is that of the gentle, inward motion of God's spirit teaching and comforting:

... when assembled, the great work of one and all ought to be to wait upon God, and returning out of their own thoughts and imaginations, to feel the Lord's presence and know a "gathering into his Name" indeed, where he is "in the midst" according to his promise. And as every one is thus gathered, and so met together inwardly in their spirits as well as outwardly in their persons, there the secret power and virtue of life is known to refresh the soul, and the pure motions and breathings of God's Spirit are felt to arise. (Barclay 296)

Burden

A *burden* is the sense of an undischarged or impending spiritual duty. The following passage from Job Scott conveys very clearly the experience of feeling a burden, and living with it. This letter is to his wife Eunice, while he is on a ministerial journey, moving from meeting to meeting, and feeling the meetings' conditions along the way:

I go as heavy laden as I can well bear, most of the time; and even when not so closely stripped as at some seasons, the weight of the meetings, which I often feel for hours before they begin, as well as in them, is such as renders me almost unconversible. This kind of burden is much greater upon me than ever before this journey, under which I am fully satisfied, many times for hours before meeting, of much approaching service; and feel it as evidently, or nearly so, as when constrained to stand up. I find when truth is felt to rise, or its stream to run somewhat like a torrent, a great difficulty in keeping enough in the moderation; but in diverse other meetings, the life is so low from first to last, that I can but just find the safe steppingstones and advanced from one to another with much weakness and moderation. But even in this, if I keep as low as the seed I find peace. (Scott, Works 2: 87-88)

A burden for a concern, if rightly based in God's requiring, is not to be taken lightly, and though it comes to some one individual, all are responsible for its stewardship. The following passages depict this in different settings, one of meeting discipline, and one of individual responsibility.

Joseph Hoag's journal describes a time when he was very clear about a leading to pay a visit to the Canadian Maritimes. The meeting with which he consulted was not willing to grant permission. They thus took responsibility for this leading, and Hoag in obedience left it to their discernment. He eventually felt freed from the requirement, and was at peace about it.

I found my mind impressed from day to day with a prospect of paying a religious visit to the inhabitants of Nova Scotia and the adjoining British Provinces, and to Friends with others, generally in New England. After considering the importance of the subject for several months, the Lord gave me to see clearly that the time was come to inform Friends of my concern, which I complied with at the next monthly meeting, under a feeling sense of the greatness of the undertaking. The meeting took up the subject and appointed a committee ... they kept it along about one year without giving a decided report. At length the concern left me, as though it had never been; of this I informed the meeting. It seemed to shock the Friends who had held back; the business dropped here. I felt no more of it for more than a year, being quite easy; but those Friends who held back, were much uneasy the whole time. (Hoag 78)

Edward Hicks described a time when he came across an isolated Friend, long out of contact with a meeting, and clearly not very religious. Hicks asked him, as the only Quaker in the region, to arrange to invite people from the area to a meeting. The local Friend professed no interest in helping, and dismissed them rudely. Hicks's companion then said, "We do not wish to put thee or anybody else to any trouble or inconveniences, and are only sorry that Friends ... should be so mistaken in their man. We will therefore bid thee farewell, and pass on." The journal continues,

My friends then arose from their seats to depart, when the old man replied in substance, Stop, stop, this won't do, you are not going to throw the responsibility of the concern on my shoulders. I can't submit to it; I must see if the Methodists can't accommodate you; they like preaching as well as any. (Hicks, Memoirs 79)

Centering
to center
centered: a centered meeting or person

These terms are very common in discussions of Quaker worship and spiritual practice in our time. They connote the process of bringing one's entire being into a place of quiet attention before God; a meeting as well as an individual can be thus centered. The language of centering is not confined to Friends; for instance, the Benedictine Basil Penington's book, *Centering prayer*, is widely used among other Christians. The phrase dates back in Quaker spiritual practice at least to the late eighteenth century. One of the best ways to open a discussion among Friends about their practice of private or corporate prayer is to ask Friends to share how they "center down."

This passage from Elias Hicks's journal places *centering* in the context of a meeting, such as a yearly meeting, where Friends were having trouble focusing their attention on the Presence:

> In those large meetings, where Friends are collected from various parts, the weak and the strong together, and especially in those for worship, it is essentially necessary that Friends get inward, and wait in their proper gifts, keeping in view their standing and place in society, especially those in the ministry.
>
> For otherwise there is danger, even from a desire to do good, of being caught with the enemies' transformations, particularly with those that are young, and inexperienced; for we seldom sit in meetings but some prospect presents, which has a likeness, in its first impression, to the right thing; and as these feel naturally fearful of speaking in large meetings, and in the presence of their elderly friends, and apprehending they are likely to have something to offer, they are suddenly struck with the fear of man, and thereby prevented from centering down to their gifts, so as to discover whether it is a right motion or not. (227)

In the following passage, Joseph John Gurney writes to the eventually schismatic Isaac Crewdson (associated with the Beaconite controversy[35]),

---

35 The Beaconite controversy erupted in England with the publication by Isaac Crewdson of a book,

who is under a concern to jettison anything in Quakerism that is not shared by the current Evangelical movement. Gurney defends the meaning of these phrases, and the importance of what they point to—an awareness of the divine presence, but also as a point of orientation, or the perspective from which all of one's life and actions are evaluated.

"Creaturely exertions," "creaturely activity," thou sayest, are not Scripture phrases, and the mischief is very great of using unscriptural terms .... Such phrases also, as 'sinking down,' 'centering down,' 'digging deep,' 'dwelling deep,' 'turning inward, '... we hardly need say they are not the language of Christ and his apostles." The general principle, as regards terms, here alluded to, is unquestionable.

But allow me to express my conviction that, although these phrases are somewhat awkward, they are capable of a meaning which is deeply scriptural, and of the greatest possible importance to our religious welfare, both as individuals and as a society. The want of more depth, of more humiliation, of a more frequent descent to the well-spring of life, of a more diligent application to the all-wise Counsellor who condescends to dwell within us by his Spirit, appears to me to be one of the greatest and most characteristic dangers of the present day. May we be brought into the depths together, and there know the love and power of Christ to triumph over all our disputations, and to heal all our wounds! (Braithwaite 1: 112)

A Beacon to the Society of Friends, which, among other things, asserted the supreme authority of Scripture over other sources of guidance, including the Inward Light of Christ, thus controverting Friends' traditional testimony. A small but painful separation ensued in the Manchester area, after much effort by London Yearly Meeting to compose the disagreement, an effort in which Gurney played an important part. Elisha Bates of Ohio Yearly Meeting, an energetic sympathizer with Crewdson, expressed similar views among American Friends, still traumatized by the Great Separation of 1827.

Clear
Clearness
"I am clear"

Clear was often used by ministers when they felt that they had done all God had asked of them in a geographic area, or in a given situation.

> On first day morning we went to their meeting at Hailstown, which was largely attended by friends and others, amongst whom I had to labour in the discharge of duty; but not feeling quite clear, and the people living too distant to meet again that day, another meeting was appointed at eleven on second day morning, which was also fully attended, and proved an open, satisfactory opportunity ... (Routh 76-7)

Perhaps the most famous use of this word is by George Fox in his last days.

> The 11th day of the 11th month [January], and the first day of the week, he was at Gracechurch Street meeting, where he declared a long time very preciously and very audibly and went to prayer.... Thence he went to ... a Friend's house in Whitehart Court near the meetinghouse. And he said he thought he felt the cold strike to his heart as he came out of the meeting, but was pretty cheery with Friends that came to him there, and said, "I am glad I was there. Now I am clear, I am fully clear." (Journal 759)

Friends would often seek to *be clear* or to have *clearness* about a leading before following it, and modern Friends have used the process of seeking clearness in many cases where an individual is facing a decision whose spiritual dimensions they wish to explore with a few Friends. Although clearness committees have some very recent features, Friends have always found value in the prayerful, loving, and often challenging counsel of a few from their community.

Close
Close work

"I had close work" meant that a minister was required by the Spirit to say difficult, embarrassing, or reprimanding things during a meeting or in a message during an opportunity in someone's home. The root of this meaning may be glimpsed in a passage in Martha Routh's journal, when she describes how "close travel" was required to get to the next stop on her journey. The meaning seems to be that the travelers kept hard on their task, taking little break, and attending carefully to an uncertain path, in order to reach their haven before nightfall.

In light of this nuance, *close* work may have originally meant "attentive" work, as in staying close to the Guide, despite the knowledge that what was being said was possibly difficult or upsetting to hear. Of course, there are also echoes of this word in the current phrase "close to home," in the sense of "uncomfortably near to the truth."

> We went straightaway to the friend and laid the case before him in a very close manner too tedious to mention to the full and we strove with him for to get him in the mind to go again with us to that place where that separation was together with his wife and a friend or two to interpret. (Morris 53)

> At a meeting at Langtree which proved a close yet thorough good meeting. We were both led to speak home to those who had known the truth and had fell from it and to divers other states as they open to us. 21st at a meeting at Ashton in which was hard work but favored to divide the word. There was a word of consolation to the heavy hearted in Zion, encouragement for them were seeking the right way of the Lord, as well as reproof for the backsliders in Israel. (Hudson 186)

> Parting in tenderness, we returned to Amesbury, 7 miles, had a meeting there on third day, a time of close labor, being dipped into several states, yet relievingly so, and my mind was favored to feel quiet poverty. (Routh 96)

... we set their meeting on fifth day, and had to labor in the gospel in a close awakening manner, much the relief of my own mind, which it felt secretly weary and heavy laden. (Routh 170)

Comfortable, uncomfortable

Comfortable or *uncomfortable* refer to a sense—sometimes tentative, sometimes quite definite—that the will of God is—or is not— being attended to, usually in a business meeting. Such feelings can occur at any time, causing a Friend (especially the uncomfortable one) to seek the reason. (See also *easy, uneasy*). The journals frequently refer to meetings as comfortable, or uncomfortable, times.

My wadings have been much in the deeps of exercise and want; yet, through favour, have had divers blessed and comfortable meetings. (Scott, Works 2: 38)

Concern
(A concern was upon me)

A *concern* is a burden placed by God upon a person. Typically, if it is a true concern and not simply a good idea, the person will not be *easy* until they have done all that the concern requires, even at great expense of time and effort. In many cases, a minister was liberated (given the freedom) by the meeting to carry out the concern.

I sat in our meeting today under much exercise and concern that I might not withhold anything given to me for others. Some having expressed concern, and wonder that my mouth is so generally closed in our meetings for worship. I clearly saw that I might arise under a great weight of exercise, which this day as well as at many other times, has impressed my mind; that we as a people, once eminently favored to experience heavenly good, like more and more seek portability to worship God in spirit and in truth, feeling strong desires in my heart that the life and power of religion might be duly sought after, believing if this was the case, we would feel our heavenly Father's presence among us. (Branson 57)

Twelfth of sixth month being the first of the week and a rainy day, we continued in our tent, and I was led to think on the nature of the exercise which hath attended me. Love was the first motion, and thence a concern arose to spend some time with the Indians, that I might feel and understand their life and the spirit they live in, if haply I might receive some instruction from them, or they might be in any degree helped forward by my following the leadings of truth among them. (Woolman 156)

Condition
Speak to one's condition

Condition or *state* refers to the situation of a person's (or a meeting's) spiritual character and way of life. Discerning ministers were often led to speak quite accurately about the *state* or *condition* of one person, and sometimes of an entire meeting. Even today some yearly meetings still ask subordinate meetings to prepare an annual "state of the meeting" report, sometimes referred to as a report on the meeting's "spiritual condition."

On first days, I frequented meetings, and the greater part of my time I slept, but took no account of preaching, nor received any other benefit, than being there kept me out of bad company.... and thus I went on for about three years; but one first-day, being at meeting, a young woman named Anne Wilson was there, and preached; she was very zealous, and fixing my eye upon her, she with a great zeal pointed her finger at me, uttering these words with much power: "A traditional Quaker, thou comest to meeting as thou went from it the last time, and goest from it as thou came to it, but art no better for thy coming, what wilt thou do in the end?" This was so pat to my then condition, that, like Saul, I was smitten to the ground, as it might be said. (Bownas, An Account 3)

In the 1700s, *speaking to conditions* carried an additional connotation when used in reference to ministers traveling under concern. Occasionally in public worship, but very often in private or family *opportunities* (see in glossary below), ministers were (are) led to articulate some insight about problems, dilemmas, or developing potentials in one or more persons present. The minister may understand the import or relevance of such messages, but might never know their impact. Unfortunately, there is danger that the minister might formulate messages like this, instead of relying divine guidance. Conscientious ministers do their best not to get background information about people before visits, and eschew gossip as much as possible. Commitment to saying only what is truly called for is one important source of the challenge and labor of opportunities. When the minister presumes to speak to conditions because it seems expected, or does so out of habit or over-anxiousness, it leaves an unclean feeling not to be forgotten by the sensitive soul.

> If [this speaking to conditions] is not done humbly, sincerely, and courageously, the result may be to damage the faith of both of you. It may lessen respect for the idea of opportunities, and the experience of prayer; and may also lessen respect for you, the visitor. Our faith is weak enough, in these days, that we should be very careful of damaging it with anything fake. John William Graham wrote, "I have once experienced this family sitting from an American Friend in my youth. I regret to say that it was all wrong in my case, and I thought it was pretence. The gift cannot be had by routine. (Drayton, *On living* 144, quoting Graham, *Psychical Experiences* 34)

Convinced

Friends tend to use *convinced* rather than *converted* to describe someone's joining the Quaker movement. The state of *convincement* is an early but important step, which occurs when one first accepts Quakerism as a path of truth, a first conscious commitment. This then is followed by a period of weeks or months or years before full conversion of mind and behavior is achieved (if ever). Friends thus will say that *convincement* is an event, but *conversion* may be a lifelong process. Brian once overheard a young person raised in a Quaker household saying, "I am a Friend by upbringing, but now I hope by convincement, too." See also the discussion of *sanctification*, discussed in the main text.

William Dewsbury was the first yt published truth in the Lower Side of the county [Bedfordshire]. And many was Convinced and Readyly Recd [received] the Truth in ye Love of itt; and Great was the Gathering in that day, both of old & young, in so much yt truth's testemony had a good Efect, upon the hearts of Male and Female.[sic] (*First Publishers of Truth* 6)

[In 1654] Tho. Stacy, Tho. Stubs, wth several More as Jams Lancaster, and Richd Hubathorn, ware [were] ye ffirst yt published ye truth in ye Vper Side of ye Country [Bedfordshire]... and some ware in part convinced...and ware Ready to Receive ye Testemony of Truth and Gosple Glad tideings as the Messengers ware to bring itt, and did not much consult with fflesh & Blood, but Soon putt in practise ye Doctrine of ye Cross, And in Measure became obedient to itt in word and in action, yt soon After Convinced, Met together...when but fiue [five] or six in Number, to wait upon god in Sillence, and ye Lorde blesd us with his presence, and Gave vs ye spirritt of Descerning, that in Measure the Ear tasted words, as the Pallett Meat. [Sic] (*First Publishers of Truth* 6)

Covered meeting
A covering over the meeting

A *covered* meeting is one in which the Spirit of God so "covers" the meeting that all (or most) worshipers feel the Peace and the Presence. Such meetings may be quite silent—although rich—or they may include vocal messages, prayer, or song.

This quotation from John Woolman conveys the root of the term:

While I silently ponder on that change wrought in me, I find no language equal to convey to another a clear idea of it. I looked upon the works of God in this visible creation, and an awfulness covered me. My heart was tender and often contrite, and universal love to my fellow-creatures increased in me. (Woolman 29)

> Yearly meeting is over, and ended under as solemn a covering as I ever knew one. The holy oil swam atop of all. The Lord's name was exalted; his people's souls greatly tendered and refreshed. It was a time not to be forgotten. (Scott, Works 2: 121)

Creaturely
of the creature
creaturely activity
creaturely concerns

Creature is related to 'created'; thus, *creaturely* is anything which comes only from the part of a person that is not in touch with, or not yet in harmony with, God. Friends across the centuries have had varying degrees of suspicion of *creaturely* ideas or activities that seem to come from the surface mind. *Creaturely activities* also referred to following the conventions, fashions, and ambitions of the world. These terms occur in several quotations in the glossary.

> We had five meetings in Narragansett, and went thence to Newport on Rhode Island. Our gracious Father preserved us in an humble dependence on him through deep exercises that were mortifying to the creaturely will. (Woolman 107)

Dualistic thinking, in which *creaturely* or *"natural"* equals "imperfect" or "liable to sin" has many nuances within Quakerism (and beyond). The contrast has been drawn since Greek times between that which is material and changeable (and therefore unreliable and partial) and that which is eternal and non-material. See Matthew 10:28 and 1 Corinthians 13 for New Testament appearances of such thinking. Dualist thinking occurs widely in early Quaker writings, even in the title of a Nayler tract: "A Discovery of the First Wisdom from beneath and the Second Wisdom from above, or The Difference Betwixt the Two Seeds The One after the Flesh, the Other after the Spirit" (in *Works* 1: 42).

Yet Friends have also had a clear sense of the goodness of creation, the important place of the *creatures* in God's vision, and in our spiritual economy and development. From early in his life, George Fox preached the importance of the right use of the *creatures*, and when once he was offered a pipe by a flippant youth, Fox put it to his mouth, lest the youth think that Fox "had not unity with the creation." Thomas Clarkson, not a Quaker, reports in his *Portraiture of Quakerism* that the Friends he knew in the early 1800s demonstrated an appreciation for the *creatures*— family life, gardens and nature, good food—as long as they were under appropriate regulation by attention to the guidance of the Holy Spirit. The spiritual work is to be aware that one's organism has its own imperatives and inclinations, and that in their vividness or urgency can appear to be moved with the force of the Divine spirit, when they are not so. The conundrums created by incarnation remain with us always.

Cross
Take up the Cross
in the Cross
(see discussion in the main text)

George Fox and later Friends saw the Cross as signifying a giving up of the personal will for instead living day by day, moment by moment, in the will of God. One might say that *living in the Cross* involves a conversion from self-willfulness to willing that which is in harmony with God. In other words, a very strong human will is needed, but as we give up egotism, we all the more need what psychology calls ego strength.

> I can tell thee, it was no small cross to me to deny myself the gratification of dancing, and some other vain amusements of like nature. But when I did give them up, Oh! the peace which flowed in my soul as I travelled on in the way of self-denial! It was like the flowings of a gentle stream of joy unspeakable and full of glory. And the wish I have for thee, dear child is that thou may witness in the secret of thy own soul the flowings of the same celestial joy and consolation; which if ever thou does witness, though wilt find it is in the way of the cross to thy natural inclinations; for the cross of Christ is the alone way to the crown of glory. (Scott, Works 2: 16)

Cumber

Our word *cumbersome* comes from *cumber*, meaning unnecessary baggage, or burden. In a spiritual sense, *cumber* is anything (whether mental preoccupation or actual possessions) that burdens one from being able to commune freely with God, or to be obedient to the Divine leadings. The following passage from John Woolman's *Journal* is probably the most famous instance of this word:

> Having now been several years with my employer, and he doing less in merchandise than heretofore, I was thoughtful about some other way of business, perceiving merchandise to be attended with much cumber in the way of trading in these parts. My mind, through the power of truth, was in a good degree weaned from the desire of outward greatness, and I was learning to be content with real conveniences, that were not costly, so that a way of life free from much entanglement appeared best for me, though the income might be small. I had several offers of business that appeared profitable, but I did not see my way clear to accept of them, believing they would be attended with more outward care and cumber than was required of me to engage in. (35)

Discernment

Discernment refers to clarity about the will or the leading of God in a given situation; or an ability to know the difference between leadings of the Spirit of God and leadings from other sources. This term is not unique to Friends, being important in other traditions, for example, in the *Spiritual exercises* of Ignatius of Loyola, the founder of the Society of Jesus. In recent years, *discernment* has also come to mean the work that a Friend, committee, or meeting may do to understand the rightly ordered course of action. (See also *feel, feeling*.)

> In the love of money and in the wisdom of this world, business is proposed, then the urgency of affairs push forward, and the mind cannot in this state discern the good and perfect will of God concerning us. (Woolman 175)

In such cases I am to retire and fear before the Lord, and wait upon him for a clear discerning and sense of his truth, in the unity and demonstration of his spirit, with others who are of him and see in him. (Scott, Works 2: 247)

Here Scott quotes Isaac Penington. This is an interesting example of a nineteenth century Friend in dialogue, so to speak, with a Friend of kindred spirit from another time.

I know what I say, and moreover know, as well as I know thy face from another man's, that rightly believing thus on him, and hearkening to his teachings, leads to great and glorious discoveries, and to a very clear discernment of the states of individuals and meetings, [even though] entire strangers. (Scott, Works 2: 211)

Divine requiring
the Lord's requiring

Passages including these phrases illustrate times in which the narrator experienced sensitivity to divine presence and active guidance. *Divine requiring* often implies a very specific task to be undertaken at a particular point in time. The passages suggest that the difference between a small requirement that lasts moments is not different in essence from a call to some great work.

Today when my heart was lifted up in silent supplication on his behalf, my cousin A. B. arose on his feet and uttered a few words which affected me to tears; fully believing it was the Lord's requiring, and though at the time rather unexpected to me. (Branson 105)

I am thankful that I was so subjected as to do the Lord's will in my small measure, for sure I am that is the reasonable duty of all the Lord's people to be obedient to his requirings in all things even unto death if they accept the crown of life, although it be in little things, for those who are not faithful in little things are not like to be favored with great rewards of true peace. (Morris 69)

Drawing, Draft

Friends often speak of feeling *drawn* towards a place or people. It is the first intimation of a concern or leading to visit. Often these *drafts* or *drawings* are noticed long before a definite duty is felt. The term reflects the heightened awareness of a soul that has been tendered, and made attentive to something in prayer.

> Eighth month, 1761.—Having felt drawings in my mind to visit Friends in and about Shrewsbury, I went there, and was at their Monthly Meeting, and their first-day meeting; I had also a meeting at Squan, and another at Squanquam, and, as way opened, had conversation with some noted Friends concerning their slaves. I returned home in a thankful sense of the goodness of the Lord. (Woolman 117)

Easy
uneasy
(see also comfortable, uncomfortable)

One is *easy* if one's inward peace is not disturbed by a sense of duty (to be undertaken) or reproof (for a duty neglected). One may also be *easy with* a course of action if no *stop* or inward warning against it is perceived.

> As to my little testimony at Purchase, I have for several days been easy and satisfied that it might all be well, though when I wrote before, I being under the very hour and power of darkness, as it were, every suggestion of the doubtful kind, was like a fiery dart of the adversary. (Scott, Works 2: 28)

Exercise
under exercise
exercise of spirit
weighty exercise of the mind

Exercise is a state of being deeply moved or stirred in spirit.

Of late years a deep exercise hath attended my mind, that Friends may dig deep, may carefully cast forth the loose matter and get down to the rock, the sure foundation, and there hearken to that Divine voice which gives a clear and certain sound. (Woolman 184)

For several weeks after my arrival, when my mouth was opened in meetings, it was like the raising of a gate in a water-course when a weight of water lay upon it. In these labors there was a fresh visitation to many, especially to the youth; but sometimes I felt poor and empty, and yet there appeared a necessity to appoint meetings. In this I was exercised to abide in the pure life of truth, and in all my labors to watch diligently against the motions of self in my own mind. (Woolman, Whittier, ed., 36 Journal 270-271)

Sometimes *exercise* can refer to the content on which a meeting is focused, whether in worship or business. The clerk may seek to draft a minute of the meeting's exercise, as a way to support the meeting's better deliberation.

What is a Minute of Exercise? A minute of exercise expresses the clerk's sense of the condition of the meeting after some time spent in corporate discernment. It seeks to identify how the spirit seems to have moved through the body in an emerging concern, or by pointing towards work that the meeting feels it should take up again, or seeking further clarity. It is not a record of each message voiced or of a debate, nor does it seek to reflect the whole process by which the meeting has arrived at the point when the minute is taken. It may be a kind of log book, a milestone, and a sign post: thus far we have been led, as we seek to know God's will; we have a sense of where we might seek for the opening way, and we may note certain issues, openings, gifts, or blessings that we wish to bear in mind as we fare forward. (New England Yearly Meeting of Friends, *2010 minutes.* http://www.neym.org/sessions2010/sessions.neym.org/minutes-of-exercise.html.)

---

36 All references to Woolman's journal refer to the Moulton edition, except where indicated, such as here.

Feel
Felt, felt led, felt called
felt (I was required) to go
(see also discernment)
(this term is addressed in the main text)

Feel, as often used by traditional Friends, suggests a sense of divine leading to speak or act, or a sense of discernment about a person or situation. It is, however, important to note the difference between this use of *feeling* as discernment and the conventional use of *feeling* as referring to emotional states.

Gathered
gathered meeting
to gather

When a meeting is *gathered,* the sense of God's presence is felt and shared because worshiping Friends are available to the Teacher. A *gathered meeting* describes a meeting that has centered, or in which all the various individuals and their diverse thoughts feel that they are part of one body, drawn together by Christ. This was eloquently described by Thomas Kelly in his essay, "The Gathered Meeting." With the term *gathered*, there are connotations of a scattered flock being collected into safety by the shepherd, and coming under the shepherd's control; and "scattered" is a term also sometimes used to describe a meeting's condition. But *gathered* also can also be used to describe the condition of individuals who are focused and ordered by the Spirit.

> I crossed the Susquehanna, and coming among people in outward ease and greatness, supported chiefly on the labor of slaves, my heart was much affected, and in awful retiredness my mind was gathered inward to the Lord, humbly desiring that in true resignation I might receive instruction from him respecting my duty among this people. (Woolman 149)

> O my Friends! Feel your minds gathered into a sense of God's love, into a pure exercise of His heavenly life and love, that in this we may go on and travel together; that in this you may be exercised together, for the glory

of God, and the good and peace and welfare of one another. (Francis Stamper, in Burns and Wallace 254)

The natural man loveth eloquence, and many love to hear eloquent orations, and if there be not a careful attention to the gift, men who have once labored in the pure gospel ministry, growing weary of suffering, and ashamed of appearing weak, may kindle a fire, compass themselves about with sparks, and walk in the light, not of Christ, who is under suffering, but of that fire which they in departing from the gift have kindled, in order that those hearers who have left the meek, suffering state for worldly wisdom may be warmed with this fire and speak highly of their labors. That which is of God gathers to God, and that which is of the world is owned by the world. (Woolman, Worship 29)

Phoebe Doncaster once described John Stephenson Rowntree, a prominent Friend of the nineteenth century, enjoying a moment of humor in family settings:

It was delightful to see the smile break out on his grave face accompanied by kindling eyes and deepening colour ... as he looked into your eyes for response and sympathy, till the amusement subsided, and his usual "gathered" expression returned.... [for him] the word "gathered" was often chosen to describe a calm and collected state of mind, or way of doing things, paying visits, for example, and it represented a kind of ideal to be aimed at. (Doncaster 76-7)

Gospel Order, ordering of the Gospel

Gospel order can refer to the process for handling differences as described in Matthew 18:15-17. It can also describe the good order that results in a community from careful and courageous attention to the Light, which harmonizes the gifts of the community, and nourishes spiritual growth.[37]

---

37 See Sandra Cronk, Gospel Order: *A Quaker Understanding of Faithful Church Community*, Walling-

Early on in the Quaker movement, it was felt clearly that old systems of hierarchical control were not appropriate for a community under the immediate guidance of the living Christ. Yet the freedom of the Gospel was still constrained by the guidance of that same Spirit of truth and love, the Spirit of the God who gave law.

William Dewsbury wrote in 1653:

> This is the Word of the Living God to his Church he hath called and chosen … to place his Name into order, and guide in his pure Wisdom…. That in every particular Meeting of Friends, Servants and Children of the most high God, that there be chosen from among you, one or two who are most grown in the Power and Life, in the pure discerning in the Truth, to take the care and charge over the Flock of God, in that place; and this is the Word of the living God to you who are chosen … not to rule as Lorders over God's Heritage, but rule in the Power of the Spirit in all purity, to be examples to the Flock, and to see that order be kept in the Church. (Dewsbury 1)

The Spirit, if attended to, would order events in a meeting for worship, so that there was a right use of individuals' gifts, for their own and the people's benefit. It is painful to recognize when one has interfered with others' worship by inattention to the Spirit's direction, whether by speaking too much or soon, or being too hesitant.[38]

> … through my backwardness I sat under the burden of the word so long that the proper time slipped in which should I have stood up which was a hurt to both myself and the meeting and I believe made hard work for my companion, for where there is not a

---

ford, PA: Pendle Hill Publications, 1991 and Lloyd Lee Wilson, *Essays on the Quaker vision of Gospel Order,* Wallingford, PA: Pendle Hill Publications, 1993 for sensitive explorations of the fundamentals of this dimension of Gospel order.

38 For more on this, see Samuel Bownas, *A description of the qualifications necessary to a Gospel minister,* Wallingford, PA: Pendle Hill Publications, 1989 [edited re-issue, first published 1750], William P. Taber, "Quaker ministry: the inward motion and the razor's edge," and Drayton, *On living with a concern for Gospel ministry.*

keeping our ranks each in our own line of duty, it flings the whole out of joint and the meeting seldom if ever recovers when thus the gospel property is invaded.

I have oft compared the ministry to a fountain or spring of water and ministers to pipes through which the water is conveyed to diverse parts of the city, some greater some lesser, according to the distance the stream is to be conveyed ... and very frequently we see one pipe so fixed as to be in some sort dependent on another and of any impediment happens to either it frustrates the grand design of conveyance, and no pipe so small or minute but there is some service or part to act and it's not acting that part may possibly so disconcert the whole as to incommode a great part if not the whole of the city. (Hudson 157)

For Fox, the idea of *gospel order* grew as he came to see God at work in ordering and regulating at every level, from the individual to the cosmos. Most often, *gospel order* is that organization of a person's life, or of a meeting's life, which grows out of being (dwelling) in the Truth. Gospel, as used here, refers not only to the words and example of the written gospels, but also to the Power of the Gospel. One could not have the Power of the Gospel, said Fox, unless one lived in the Cross.

You that are come to know the truth ... come to know the Order of Life, so that all things may be kept in that sweet Order and government, to the Glory of God, the refreshment of all, a sweet savor to God, in the hearts of all people.... My desire is ... that the joyful and glorious Order of the everlasting Gospel, all may be in possession of. So that in the Light, Spirit, and Power you may all have a care of God's Glory, his honor and his Church's Peace, keeping in the Unity of his everlasting Spirit. (Fox, Epistle 264)

Gospel order is pervasive; it is the order and harmony that characterizes every part of creation when that part is functioning according to the divine will ... it has been the experience of Friends that no part of their lives as individuals or as a faith community is separate from their vision of gospel order. (Wilson 4)

Hireling ministry

This was a term used by Friends late into the nineteenth century to refer to the paid ministers typical of other denominations. Friends believed that no true minister of the Gospel could be a "hireling," someone who ministered a learned profession (no matter how good the intention for entering upon it). The commercial connotations of the term had negative weight during the periods when tithes were required by law, and therefore Friends suffered for refusing the forced support of clergy.

The common contrasting model instead was that of the prophet, under orders from God. Alongside this, however, was the image of the parent or shepherd, someone with greater maturity or a wider point of view, carrying the responsibility for the care and nurture of others in the community.

> I am the good shepherd. The good shepherd lays down his life for his sheep. The hired hand, who does not own the sheep, sees the wolf coming and leaves the sheep and runs away, and the wolf snatches them and scatters them. (John 10:11-12)

In more recent Quaker language, *hireling ministry* is less frequent, although separations over the principle of the "free ministry" (or "free Gospel Ministry") continued to the threshold of the 20th century. Underlying issues related to ministry as calling and as profession remain to this day within the Society.

> The testimony at Athy was much by way of opening the deceits, worldly-mindedness, and want of real gospel qualification, in those hireling teachers, who...are the 'blind leaders of the blind.' (Scott, Journal 350)

Friends are encouraged also to consider the challenge in A.N. Brayshaw's words:

> We do well to remember that even if the preaching of certain "paid" ministers is mechanical or superficial, there is many a one who, knowing a sermon will be required of him, looks forward to it in the spirit of prayer and love for his congregation, of watchfulness over his lower self

and of expectation of power, so that when the appointed time comes it is right for him to give his message. Our way of worship and conception of ministry give no excuse for our prayer and love, our watchfulness and expectation being less than his. (The Things 36)

Lamb's war

Early Friends saw themselves engaged in a spiritual warfare—the war of the gentle but conquering Lamb (Jesus, as described in the book of Revelation)—against all the forces of sin, evil, and pride. Although at first it may be experienced as a process of personal purification, the inward struggle against "the Man of Sin" sooner or later leads us to engage outwardly with the powers of culture, custom, and the over-reliance on human reason and competence. The Lamb that suffers conquers not only the inward kingdom, but moves ultimately to transform the society that is a fruit of the human heart. Can the process work in the other direction —starting first with an outcry against injustice or evil in the world, which then leads to a realization that we ourselves are in need of inward healing and cleansing, guidance and light, if we are to continue towards integrity? Perhaps so; but we cannot proceed far towards that integrity unless we earnestly seek towards the Light, and allow ourselves to be empowered by it.

> The end of his war is, to judge [the] deceiver openly before all the creation showing that his ways, fashions, and customs are not what God ordered for man to live in, in the beginning; to bind him and to redeem...out of his captivity all who will believe in the Lamb and are weary of this service and bondage to his enemy, and who will but come forth and give their names and hearts to join with him and bear his image and testimony openly before all men; ...and all that follow him to redeem them to God. (Nayler 4: 2)

Libertine Spirit

This term referred to a Friend or anyone living in liberty to the judgment and desires of their individual will, and avoiding the restrictions of traditional Quakerism, which were assumed to be the restrictions and boundaries necessary to remain under the governance and freedom of the Spirit. John Woolman recounts his efforts to separate himself from the loose companions of his youth:

> I was visited by several young people, my former acquaintance, who knew not but vanities would be as agreeable to me now as ever; and at these times I cried to the Lord in secret for wisdom and strength, for I felt myself encompassed with difficulties and had fresh occasion to bewail the follies of time past in contracting a familiarity with a libertine people. (30)

Life
"in the Life"
"the message had life in it"
(discussed fully in main text)

Life is most often synonymous with "the presence and power of the Holy Spirit."

> The yearly meeting here has been large and solid; much more in truth's life and authority than I expected; or the mournful state of the ministry gave me a gloomy prospect in regard to the yearly meeting. There is much preaching in England, but too little of gospel. There are many teachers, but few fathers. A few sound elders here and there, are preserved; but too many in that station delight in the sound, crave eagerly to be fed by the ears, and scarce know how to endure silence; and often, very often my business has been to starve them, not being able to utter one word in the life of the gospel. (Scott, Works 2: 191)

Love, Gospel love, the love of God

This term is rooted in the passages about love in John's Gospel and letters, in which is the core of Jesus' message, his "new commandment" to his friends to love each other as he loved them (John 15:12). This "agape love" is the desire for the spiritual health of the other, and a commitment to act to forward that health whenever God opens a way to do so. Woolman catches the core of it when in his journal he speaks of those drawn to the ministry in "a lively operative desire for the good of others" (31).

Gospel love is a motivating power in and of itself. Many ministers were motivated to travel to visit families or meetings in Gospel love, with no other particular message. Moreover, love should be at the bottom or core of every concern.

> Feeling the spring of gospel love flow towards them, I inquired if there was a place where a meeting could be had with them next evening; to which the friend readily resigned his own house, and took care to have general notice given. (Routh 233)

> On the evening of the 18th I was at their meeting, where pure gospel love was felt, to the tendering of some of our hearts. The interpreters endeavored to acquaint the people with what I said, in short sentences, but found some difficulty, as none of them were quite perfect in the English and Delaware tongues, so they helped one another, and we labored along, Divine love attending. Afterwards, feeling my mind covered with the spirit of prayer, I told the interpreters that I found it in my heart to pray to God, and believed, if I prayed aright, he would hear me; and I expressed my willingness for them to omit interpreting; so our meeting ended with a degree of Divine love. (Woolman 133)

Monitor
Divine monitor
Inward monitor

Monitor literally means "one who warns," and is a synonym for *Inward guide* or *Inward Christ*. The Quaker usage is thus reminiscent of Socrates' "daimon," the inward voice which warned him against doing wrong.

> Had I steadily obeyed the truth in my inward parts; had I attended singly and faithfully to this divine monitor, my portion had been peace; my cup, a cup of consolation. (Scott, Journal 15)

My strongest predilection was for literature, and I read with avidity almost every work that came in my way, except those that were considered pernicious, and even some of this class occasionally shared my attention, notwithstanding the repoofs of that Divine monitor which pleads with us in the secret of the soul, and condemns for sin. (Janney 8)

Motion
inward motion
felt a motion to....
Move, moved

A *motion* is a subtle inward action of the Spirit that points to a specific message in a meeting, or to any act, such as asking for a special meeting or permission to travel in the ministry.

The Spirit of Christ, by which we are guided, is not changeable, so as once to command us from a thing as evil, and again to move unto it. (Fox Journal 399)

Travelling up and down of late, I have had renewed evidences that to be faithful to the Lord, and content with his will concerning me, is a most necessary and useful lesson for me to be learning; looking less at the effects of my labor than at the pure motion and reality of the concern, as it arises from heavenly love. (Woolman 72)

Twelfth of sixth month being the first of the week and rainy day, we continued in our tent, and I was led to think on the nature of the exercise which hath attended me. Love was the first motion, and thence a concern arose to spend some time with the Indians, that I might feel and understand their life and the spirit they live in, if haply I might receive some instruction from them, or they might be in any degree helped forward by my following the leadings of truth among them; and as it pleased the Lord to make way for my going at a time when the troubles of war were increasing, and when, by reason of much wet weather, travelling was more difficult than usual at that season, I looked upon it as a more favorable opportunity to season my mind, and to bring me into a nearer sympathy with them. As mine eye was to the great Father of Mercies, humbly desiring to learn his will concerning me, I was made quiet and content. (Woolman 127)

Nudge

This term has become more frequent among Friends in the past few years, and though it is mostly synonymous with "leading," *nudge* lays emphasis upon the often very small and tentative beginnings of some spiritual development. A nudge is gentle, and often does not convey its ultimate meaning clearly; meaning may unfold as the path unfolds. Discernment is the essential tool for cultivation of these tender shoots. One Friend has listed some key signs of authenticity of a *nudge* or leading:

1. It leads to love and light. 2. It comes with clarity, or grows in clarity as it is lived with; 3. It resonates with deep desires; 4. It is not ego-driven; 5. It is persistent; 6. It is in harmony with Jesus. 7. It is confirmed by others. 8. It leads into service to others. 9. It requires rest. 10. It leads to more love and joy. (Fardelmann, Nudged xxi-xxiv)

Open, an Opening

Open (1)

Opening can refer to a direct revelation about some aspect of religious reality. An *opening* would usually come as a sudden, unexpected, intuitive understanding. Such *openings* often—but not always—involved a deeper understanding of Scripture. In the first generation of Friends, this language was particularly characteristic of George Fox and of those convinced by him. Hugh Barbour suggests, however, that others who had come to the Quaker position independently did not speak of openings in this way ("Openings").

The Lord showed me that such as were faithful to him in the power and light of Christ, should come up into that state in which Adam was before he fell, in which the admirable works of creation, and the virtues thereof, may be known, through the openings of that divine Word of wisdom and power in which they were made. Great things did the Lord lead me into, and wonderful depths were opened unto me, beyond what can by words be declared; but as people come into subjection to the spirit of God, and grow up in the image and power of the Almighty, they may receive the Word of wisdom that opens all things, and come to know the hidden unity in the Eternal Being. (Fox 27-8)

... we grew more and more into an understanding of Divine Things and Heavenly Mysteries, through the Openings of the Power that was daily among us, and wrought sweetly in our Hearts (Burnyeat 11)

Open (2)

Another common meaning of the word *open* is to explain the spiritual signification of something (for example, of Scripture).

William Penn writes of George Fox:

He had an extraordinary gift in opening the Scriptures. He would go to the marrow of things, and show the mind, harmony, and fulfilling of them with much plainness, and to great comfort and edification. (58)

The prototype for this meaning of *open* is likely to be Luke 24:30-32:

And it came to pass, as he sat at meat with them, he took bread, and blessed it and brake it, and gave to them. And their eyes were opened and they knew him; and he vanished out of their sight. And they said one to another, Did not our hearts burn within us while he talked with us by the way and while he opened to us the Scriptures?

Open (3) "unconstrained"

Some use *open* to describe the feeling of a setting, such as a time of worship, in which there is a spiritual mood of freedom and bounty. The atmosphere enables a ministering Friend to speak with no hesitation, anxiety, or hindrance in the spirit of the meeting.

> 29th to Morley where my companion had an extraordinary open opportunity but I was deeply dipped into suffering which often filled to my lot. (Hudson 187)

> Through the dedication of my dear companion, getting up to the pointings of duty, the door got a little open for my standing on my feet; and through unmerited mercy, strength was given to preach the gospel to the poor, and to exalt the testimony of truth, above all opposition. (Hudson 257)

> ... a very large gathering, and, through the renewed extendings of holy help, was an open time of labor, tending greatly to the relief of my oppressed mind. (Routh 182)

As with many of these phrases, there are times when some or all connotations might be present:

> Early did I feel there were dark, opposing spirits of the meeting; but patiently seeking for the renewings of holy help, my mind became raised above all fear, within or without, and I humbly trust counsel was opened, and strength afforded to communicate it to the people in the wisdom of truth. (Routh 96)

Opportunity

An *opportunity* was (is) a meeting for worship held between two people or a small group of people outside of the regular meeting time. The place was usually in a home, but it could be anywhere. Sometimes the word was used for the meetings (or "sittings") that some traveling ministers held in Quaker homes in each area they visited. The word could be used to refer to a meeting between two or more Friends when one had a disagreement with the other, or when one sought spiritual counsel from another. The word could also refer to a spontaneous silence that might suddenly come to a group of Friends in a living room, or even at a meal.

The essential insight of *opportunity* is that anytime one makes room for an encounter with the living God, something may happen, whether refreshment, healing, reproof, insight, clarity, comfort, or commission. The simple act of requesting, offering, or stumbling into a time of worship is the opening of a door into the divine life.

> We set forward for Lymington, 20 miles; dined at a friend's house, who had lately joined the society by convincement, had a religious opportunity in the family; and then proceeded on our way. (Routh 84)

> The meeting was fully attended by those of other societies, and, through the renewings of best help, was in some degree a satisfactory opportunity, but I believe would have been more so, if the slow gathering of the people had not interrupted silent worship. (Routh 90)

> Friends met to finish their business, and then the meeting for worship ensued, which to me was a laborious time; but through the goodness of the Lord, truth, I believed, gained some ground, and it was a strengthening opportunity to the honest-hearted. (Woolman 67)

Plain, plainness
going plain, plain dress and speech and lifestyle

Plainness is an outward statement of simplicity. Frances Taber states the essentials beautifully:

> The taproot of simplicity is to be found at that point in the life of a Friend when the realization comes that his or her inner and outer lives are connected, that for the inward life to continue to grow, there must be a response from the outward life. It is at that point where awareness dawns that spiritual knowledge itself comes from an open relationship between one's inner and outer lives, and from a free movement between the two. (F. Taber, *Finding the taproot* 6)

Plainness carries many nuances, including clothing, furnishings, lifestyle, or directness of speech. The language is famously characterized by "thee" and "thou," and the disuse of day- and month-names with pagan origins, substituting numbers (so that "Wednesday, June 12th" becomes "Fourth Day, the 12th of 6th month"). Plainness of speech included also disuse of honorifics (e.g. "Mr." or "Sir"), using first and last names instead, avoidance of conventional greetings (such as "How do you do?"), and carefulness to be exact in speech.

Exactness of speech is sometimes enshrined in humorous stories. For example, an aged Friend is asked if his arthritis is bothering him, and he answers, "I have a feeling akin to pain." Or, Herbert Hoover and a colleague are looking out the passenger train window. "Oh look," says his friend, "those sheep have just been shorn!" Hoover replies: "On this side, certainly." Yet the simplicity and precision of the *plain* style of speaking is often beautiful and effective in its clarity and balance.

Plain also came, in time, to imply the adoption of distinctively Quaker dress and speech. *Plainness* was never definitively defined; the *plain* dress of Fox's day was not like that of Lucretia Mott's, and from yearly meeting to yearly meeting, cultures varied (within bounds), as can be attested by examination of photographs or portraits from across the centuries.[39] Indeed, some Friends still adopt plain dress, but the details of the clothing vary considerably as in the past.

[I] Had some conversation with an individual who is under conviction that it would be right for her to use the plain language, thee and thou to one person, but [she] is evidently evading the cross, pleading the excuse that her education has been so different in her surroundings such that she finds it very hard, and the cross theory great. (Branson 59)

Fifth of fifth month, 1768.—I left home under the humbling hand of the Lord, with a certificate to visit some meetings in Maryland

---

39 Amelia Mott Gummere's 1901 study of Quaker dress through time provides abundant evidence of the way that changes through the generations in the "gay [fancy] world" were echoed—however muffled—in the "plain world" of Friends. See Gummere, *The Quaker: a study in costume*, Philadelphia: Ferris & Leach Publishers, 1901.

... On my return I felt a very comfortable relief of mind, having through Divine help labored in much plainness, both with Friends selected and in the more public meetings, so that I trust the pure witness in many minds was reached. (Woolman 151-2)

Reached
to be reached

To be *reached* originally meant to be convinced of the truth of Quakerism. The root of the idea, however, is that a word or event has brought one into consciousness of the vulnerable (*tender*), pure, and creative center of one's spiritual life.

As to the said man of God, William Dewsbury, how he was gifted it was well-known in many or most parts of the nation, and many were the living seals of the verity of his faithful testimony, of whom many are fallen asleep but some remain unto this day.... His speech was plain and powerful, reaching to the tendering and breaking of many hearts, his discerning clear and piercing, whereby many had their conditions plainly demonstrated and laid open before them, whom before he never saw.... (First Publishers of Truth 197)

... if we mutually kept to that spirit and power which crucifies to the world, which teaches us to be content with things really needful and to avoid superfluities, giving up our hearts to fear and serve the Lord, true Unity may still be preserved amongst us. And that if such who at times were under sufferings on account of some scruples of conscience, kept low and humble and in their conduct of life manifested a spirit of true charity, it would be more likely to reach the witness in others and be of more service in the church, than if their sufferings were attended with a contrary spirit and conduct. (Woolman, Worship 27)

Rode to Sandwich, New Hampshire, and attended their First-day meeting on the twenty-ninth, in which my mind was tried in a sin-gular way for me, for after sitting a considerable time, it was made known to me that the people were waiting on me, and not on the Most High; looking to me and not to the Lord, which would close my way and I must tell it to the people ... not feeling easy without doing it, I gave up, simply told them my feelings and sat down; but soon felt like a vessel pressed full, which wanted vent, and could not have it. In this suffering condition, I had to sit as long as meetings commonly hold, until the people gave up their expectation of hearing preaching, and became quiet; then my way opened in a lengthy, searching testimony, that reached the witness for God in their minds, and broke them down to a tender feeling, and an acknowledgment of the truth. Oh! may the Lord fasten the Truth in their hearts, as a nail in a sure place, and bless the service of the day to the people. (Hoag 130)

Retire
retirement
Retiredness of mind

To be *retired* could mean literally to be in one's room, or other secluded place, for the purpose of quiet waiting upon God—whether in quiet worship, active prayer, or reflective reading and writing on spiritual subjects. For example:

> Do you make a place in your daily life for inward retirement and communion with God? (*Faith and Practice* of NEYM, Query #1)

The word also reflects a state of mind, even if perhaps in the midst of daily affairs, as in the story of Loveday Hambly recounted above (Ch. 6).

> My companion having drawings on her mind, inclined to another [meeting] with the people of the town, which was large though to my apprehension to no great purpose, great I know were my sufferings in both, for when truth did not favor I could not rejoice but found peace in keeping low and retired in spirit. (Hudson 154-155)

Retirement is akin to *gathered*. The practice of *retirement*, which will vary in its logistical forms from person to person, and from one period of life to another, is a central feature of Quakerism as a living spiritual method.

Retirement is considered by the Quakers as a Christian duty. The members, therefore, of this Religious Society are expected to wait in silence, not only in their places of worship, but occasionally in their families or in their private chambers, in the intervals of their daily occupations, that in stillness of heart, and in freedom from the active contrivance of their own will, they may acquire both direction and strength for the performance of the duties of life. (Brinton, *Friends for 300 Years*, 135)

Retired meetings

In addition to public meetings, early Friends also met in *retired* meetings, where the work of the Spirit could move forward with more focus and concentration—so the work of conversion after convincement could be supported in fellowship. These meetings sometimes occurred on weekdays. Fox recommended that not all go out to "thresh the heathenish nature, " but "let Friends keep together, and wait in their own meeting place, so will the life (in the Truth) be preserved and grow" (Fox, Epistle XIV).

> We have had in other chapters to speak of the class of meetings known as "Private," "Silent," or "Retired" meetings, in which the edification of the flock, rather than the gathering in of those who were outside the pale, seems to have been the special object in view.... Frequent allusions to such meetings occur in the minutes, and they were continued all through the times when Friends were an increasing body. (Beck and Ball 226)

Throughout his life, Fox thought of these meetings as important—the minutes of the Second Day Morning Meeting of ministering Friends for November 1688 report a letter from Fox urging the establishment of more of such meetings in London. The different character and work of these meetings is reflected in this section of Fox's 1658 message to ministering Friends:

So, Friends, this is the word of the Lord God to you all, be watchful and careful in all meetings ye come into; for where Friends are sitting together in silence, they are many times gathered into their own measures.

When a man is come newly out of the world, from ministering to the world's people, he cometh out of the dirt; and then he had need take heed that he be not rash. For now, when he comes into a silent meeting, that is another state; then he must come, and feel his own spirit, how it is, when he comes to them that sit silent.

If he be rash, they will judge him, that having been in the world, and amongst the world, the heat is not yet off him. For he may come in the heat of his spirit out of the world; whereas the others are still and cool; and his condition in that not being agreeable to theirs, he may rather do them hurt, by begetting them out of the cool state into the heating state, if he be not in that which commands his own spirit, and gives him to know it. (Fox, *Journal* 340-341)

The searcher of hearts

This is a description of God actively at work.

No one knows how it has been with me for the past six months, save the Searcher of hearts. (Branson 118). See Psalm 139.

Season, seasoned, seasoning

The reader will encounter the words in this family at many points in this book. Friends have long known that just because one has a realization, or sees a solution to a problem, or feels that a leading is developing, it does not mean that the time has yet come for action. We often say that some business "needs to season" before being brought before the meeting for business. If an action is proposed, for example, to a yearly meeting session, a Friend is likely to ask, "Has this been seasoned?", that is, has it been duly considered by a subordinate meeting, or a relevant committee? *Seasoned* could also refer to something being held until it is "in its season," that is, at the time of ripeness, and not to see harvest before its time. Remember the tree, planted by the rivers of water, in Psalm 1, that brings forth its fruit in due season.

Season can also be a culinary metaphor, akin to the use of the word "savory" to mean "delightful to the Lord":

> The next day had a comfortable meeting with a few Friends in those parts. I found my spirit sweetly seasoned with a larger degree of divine love them common, which greatly enlarged my heart towards them. (Hudson 247)

State
State of the meeting
a person's state
See: condition

> After I sat down my spirit was covered with distress even to anguish, however was favored to prostrate myself at the feet of my master who knew if I heard was not owing to the wickedness of my heart, but to great readiness to grasp at vision, which is no qualification to preach for these many openings for our own instruction only, and the states of meeting revealed to us that at one time and perhaps it's for another days service and sometimes as there is sundry states in most meetings it may be that we are opened and understanding to see them, but called upon to speak but to a few. (Hudson 198)

> In these parts, it was as in many other places, such a likeness in the states of meetings, it seemed too much repetition to descend into particulars. Yet, we had this comfort, from impressions felt, that there were well concerned minds in nearly every meeting, to whom the Lord had special regard, and for whose sakes he continues his favors to the Church; and in answer to their prayers, often renews His visitations to them who are settled down at ease in a profession of the Truth, as on their beds of ivory... (Hoag 284)

A stop in the mind

A *stop in the mind* is a strong inward awareness that a given course of action should not be followed. There are many stories of Friends obeying such an "irrational" *stop*, only to find out later some very important reason for the perception.

> Until the year 1756, I continued to retail goods, besides following my trade as a tailor; about which time I grew uneasy on account of my business growing too cumbersome. I had begun with selling trimmings for garments, and from thence proceeded to sell cloths and linens; and at length, having got a considerable shop of goods, my trade increased every year, and the way to large business appeared open, but I felt a stop in my mind. (Woolman 53)

> Of late I have sometimes felt a stop in the appointment of meetings, not wholly, but in part: and I do not feel liberty to appoint them so quickly, one after another, as I have done heretofore. The work of the ministry being a work of Divine love, I feel that the openings thereof are to be waited for in all our appointments. (Woolman 325)

> After the above-mentioned visit, returned to Thomas Watsons, thinking to proceed homewards next day; but feeling myself stopped, I waited to see which way my never failing Guide would direct me; and as I kept my mind to the light, a way was opened to [several towns] to all which I went, and had a meeting at each place, which were divinely favored. (Moore 374)

Stripped, Stripping

Stripping refers to the (painful) giving up of unnecessary parts of the self, or the sense of emptiness and complete dependence on God's power.

> Tempted, tried and proven, even to an hair's breadth – what further plungings and wadings the Lord may permit me to go through, I know not; but all that I ask, all that I desire is, that my

spiritual life may be given me for a prey. Who that passes through the seasons of stripping and proving, and are again raised up with their faith and hope renewed, but can with great abasedness of self, acknowledge there is nothing in our nature, no, not a vestige or particle that can further our salvation. (Branson 62)

Tender
my heart was tendered before the Lord

To be *tender* was to be open and receptive to the spiritual reality experienced by early Friends. Other nuances of *tender* can be expressed with words like "susceptible," "sympathetic," and "teachable."

> Five lads training up for the sea were now on board this ship ... I often feel a tenderness of heart towards these poor lads, and at times look at them as though they were my children according to the flesh. Oh, that all may take heed and beware of covetousness! Oh, that all may learn of Christ who is meek and low of heart!.... Men thus redeemed will feel a tender concern for their fellow creatures and a desire that those in the lowest stations may be encouraged. (Woolman 167)

> Our labor was hard in silence but in the conclusion the little life spread over us and a number were pretty much reached and broken into tenderness and contrition. (Scott, *Journal* 138)

Tender was one of George Fox's characteristic words, and he looked for *tender* people, especially during his seeking years, whenever he came into a new place. Here follow three well-known excerpts from his journal:

> When I returned to Leicestershire, my relatives wanted me to get married; but I told them I was too young for marriage and I wished to obtain wisdom first. Others wanted me to join the auxiliary companies of the army; but I refused, and I was saddened that they proposed such things to me, being so young. Then I went to Coventry, where I took a room for awhile at a professor's house,

until people began to get acquainted with me; for there were many tender and loving people in that town. And after some time I went into my own country again, and continued about a year in great sorrow and trouble walking many nights by myself. (4-5)

About the beginning of 1647, I was moved by the Lord to go into Derbyshire, where I met with some friendly people, and had many discussions with them. Then passing into the Peak country, I met with more friendly people, and with some in empty high notions. And traveling on through some parts of Leicestershire, and into Nottinghamshire, I met with a tender people, and a very tender woman, whose name was Elizabeth Hooton. (9)

After I had received that opening from the Lord, that to be bred at Oxford or Cambridge was not sufficient to make a man a minister of Christ, I regarded the priests less, and looked more after the dissenting people. Among them I saw there was some tenderness; and many of them came afterwards to be convinced, for they had some openings. (11)

Testimony
bear testimony

A testimony is a statement consciously made (by words or by action) in support of Truth, or to be consistent with it. Thus, a Quaker sermon could be a *testimony*, or in times of persecutions, merely being an acknowledged Friend could also be a *testimony*. Silent worship, free ministry, marriage practice, and business meetings are all *testimonies*, as is the stance against oaths and war. Like the Golden Rule, many *testimonies* can be phrased as negatives or positives, and it is valuable to consider both forms, such as the *testimony* against oaths, which is part of the *testimony* for a single standard of truth; or the *testimony* against the use of the physical elements for baptism or communion, which is rooted in a commitment to the integrity of the inward and spiritual reality of these experiences of the Christian way.

All bloody principles and practices we do utterly deny, with all outward wars, and strife, and fightings with outward weapons, for any end, or under any pretence whatsoever, and this is our testimony to the whole world. (Fox 399-400)

The Lord our good God gladdened our hearts many times among friends there for many places there were not too high for truth's testimony although was through the poorest sort of his people. (Morris 55)

In regard to a message given in worship:

I thought the Lord owned the testimony he gave me to bear. (Hudson 195)

That of God in every one

This is an expression used many times by George Fox and successive generations of Friends to refer to the precious, inward Seed in each person, the witness of God, and the divine life born inwardly and grown in some measure. To this our own faithfulness in the divine life will "answer"—the connotation might suggest "resonate" with, as in a bell ringing in answer to another.

Friends,
In the power of life and wisdom, and dread of the Lord of life, and heaven and earth, dwell, that in the wisdom of God over all ye may be preserved, and be a terror to all the adversaries of God and a dread, answering that of God in them all, spreading the Truth abroad, awakening the witness, confounding deceit, gathering up out of transgression into the life, into the covenant of light and peace with God. Let all nations hear the word by sound or by writing.

Spare no place, spare not tongue, nor pen; but be obedient to the Lord God and go through the work, and be valiant for the Truth upon earth; tread and trample all that is contrary under.

Ye have the power, do not abuse it; and strength, presence, of the Lord. Eye it, and the wisdom, that with it you may all be ordered to the glory of the Lord God....

This is the word of the Lord God to you all, and a charge to you all in the presence of the living God: Be patterns, be examples in all countries, places, islands, nations, wherever you come, so that your life and conduct may preach among all sorts of people, and to them. Then you will come to walk cheerfully over the world, answering that of God in every one whereby in them ye can be a blessing and make the witness of God in them to bless you. Then to the Lord God you shall be a sweet savor, and a blessing. (Fox, Works 1: 288-9)

Truth,
owned by Truth, Scripture of Truth,
receive the Truth, live in the Truth,
for the honor of Truth
(discussed also in main text)

Truth, as used by generations of Friends, meant much more than a correct statement of fact. *Truth* was almost a synonym for God, yet it could also include the whole way of life that Friends believed they were given by Jesus, as well as the theology behind that way of life.

> When I consider that for years previous to laying this prospect before my friends, it had at times dwelt with great weight upon my mind, I wish not now to draw back from making any visit to anyone, or to any family which the truth requires... (Branson 97)

> It having pleased the Lord to draw me forth on a visit to some parts of Virginia and Carolina, you have often been in my mind; and though my way is not clear to come in person to visit you, yet I feel it in my heart to communicate a few things, as they arise in the love of truth. (Woolman 67)

> I went to Newbegun Creek, and sat a considerable time in much weakness. Then I felt Truth open the way to speak a little in much plainness and simplicity, till at length, through the increase of Divine love amongst us, we had a seasoning opportunity. (Woolman 71)

Friends, like others, have been very aware of the many ways and forms in which we encounter truth, and the corresponding duty to keep tender and teachable by that truth. When encountering apparently irreconcilable truths and underlying unity, bedrock faith often requires us to wait in patience and humility for further clarity, and in some sense to welcome the challenge.

> We cannot jump out of our human skins into God's perspective.... Part of our own Quaker witness includes urging each man to respond directly to God as he finds he is able. As long as our own truthfulness can transcend itself, we can be led back to Christ and to new truth, and are free to go forward as he leads us. Our affirmation that Christ is truth must keep us continually rethinking the meaning of scientific truths and how we may be true to our inward experience of Christ; it should also keep us endlessly open to being increasingly truthful in response to all of life and all men. (Barbour, "Christ and truth" 14)

Wait, Wait upon the Lord
(addressed fully in the main text)

When George Fox used *wait* hundreds of times in his sermons and his writings, he referred to more than a passive pause to allow time to pass. He meant it to signify an act of going very deep, of going beneath the surface reactions, fears, and pretensions until one was centered and grounded in the Divine Reality. Sometimes this waiting did indeed take time—as much as three hours, in one case— but at other times Fox's surrender into the Divine Reality occurred almost instantaneously. In the face of temptations, troubles, or persecutions he would simply *wait* in this active way. *Wait* as in "*wait* upon the Lord" also suggests service and being present with all one's attention to the slightest wish or action of the great person on whom one waits.

Watering, Watering ministry
and related terms

Friends used many metaphors to describe ministry, and *watering* is one long in use. There may be living seed among the people, but it needs nourishment to grow. A watering is gentle nourishment to the tender plants of God.

> Thomas Ralph received a part in the ministry, and had a watering testimony. (*First Publishers of Truth* 49)

> I thought to have a watering; but ye struggle so I cannot get you together. We mun have no watering tonight, I mun leave you every yan to his own Guide. (Luke Cock, in *The Friend*, vol XV, 278)

> Many things were opened, I humbly trust, in the light of truth, and under gospel authority, to the differing states of the people; yet it was a rather a season of digging and pruning, then of finding many plants ready for the watering. But I was instructively impressed, that I must be a faithful laborer in the discharge of duty, and content with my wages. (Routh 239)

Plowing, planting, and *threshing* are also used among Friends, and these terms describe spiritual work (especially ministry) that corresponds to different conditions of the people. *Plowing* suggests the preparation of the soul, an opening for planting and for nourishment: the bringing to a receptive condition. *Planting* hearkens back to the parable of the sower in the book of Luke, and betokens a teaching or way-pointing that suggests to the tendered, opened soul a spiritual possibility not suspected before. *Threshing* connotes the separation of the nourishing seed from the choking, chaffy husk. All echo Paul's comment in 1 Corinthians 3:5-7: "Who then is Paul, and who is Apollos, but ministers by whom ye believed, even as the Lord gave to every man? I have planted, Apollos watered, but God gave the increase." One cannot resist quoting Fox's epistle to ministering Friends again, where all these phrases are employed with great power and tenderness:

> Bring all into the worship of God: plow up the fallow ground, thresh and get out the corn, that all people may come to the Beginning, to Christ, who was before the world was made. For the chaff has come upon the wheat by transgression. He who treads out the chaff is out of transgression and fathoms transgression. He sees the difference between the precious and the vile and can pick out the wheat from the tares and gather it into the garner. Thus he brings the immortal soul to God, from whom it came. No one worships God but he who comes to the principle of God, which he has transgressed; no one is plowed up but he who comes to the principle of God in him, that he has transgressed. Then he does service to God, then the planting and the watering take place, and the increase comes from God. So the ministers of the spirit must minister to the spirit that has been in captivity in every one, so that with the spirit of Christ people may be led out of captivity up to God, the Father of Spirits, and do service to him, and have unity with him, with the Scriptures, and with one another. (Fox, *Journal* 263)

Weight—weighty
a weight was upon me
weighty consideration
weighty Friend

A person who has *weight* might tip the scales in a decision. Thus a *weighty* Friend is one whose spiritual discernment is much respected and valued. A *weighty* consideration is an important or solemn one. A *weight* could also be a religious concern (*burden*), or it could be a dark and oppressive feeling—as in common parlance today.

> Soon after our return ... a weighty exercise came over me, the time appearing to draw near for my paying a religious visit to Friends

in Ireland. The prospect had been opening for several years ... believing that [Martha Howarth] had something of the same kind in view, I opened my mind to her, and pointed out the season when it might be right to move, if friends united with us therein. (Routh 50)

Witness

Friends use this term in many ways that will be familiar, and at least one which is less so.

We may testify as witnesses, that is, testify as those who have first-hand experiences, of God's work or God's life as embodied in human action or community life. Such a witness acts as a guarantor of the truth of a testimony, or that a vow has been made: "Ye are my witnesses, saith the Lord, and my servant whom I have chosen; that ye may know and believe me" (Isaiah 43:10). This first-hand assertion is crucial to Christian proclamation based on experience of what eye has seen, ear has heard, and hands have handled of Christ's work within us and in the world: "the life was manifested, and we have seen it, and bear witness, and shew unto you that eternal life" (1 John 1:1-3). Friends thus act as witnesses to the truth and the law of God.

Quaker experience, however, is rooted in the experience of an inward witness, the prophetic work of Christ within, announcing first God's presence, and second God's truth in a particular context (as Paul says, God has never left us without a witness, Acts 14:17 and Romans 2:15—but we are not always ready to see or hear it). When someone or something "reaches the witness" in us, we are offered a direct encounter with the divine life. We are also provided with evidence that we can build upon as a foundation and a source of nourishment, if we heed it and allow it, in its first manifestation, to be woven into our understanding of reality, and then to act on it (having the witness in ourselves, 1 John 5:10).

What I have seen and known, heard and felt, that declare I unto you, and my witness is true, if I bore witness of myself, it were not true; but my witness stands in him, and is of him who is the light of the World.... Come to God's witness, it will abide with you; and as you abide with it, you will know its power and its leadings; be not afraid, but come to it, there's no other way to life eternal; if it bring you into trouble, it will bring you out again. (Blackborrow 52-3)

One of William Dewsbury's epistles makes use of many senses of *witness*, and may fittingly close our book:

Dear Friends, meet often together in the Name and fear of the living God, and take heed of Words; see that the Witness speaks, which will cut down your own wills, and it will minister to the Witness in others, to the slaying of their wills.

And take heed of watching over one another with an evil Eye, to spy out one another's weakness, and declare it to others, and discover [uncover] their nakedness ... but watch over one another with a pure single Eye, and if thou see the pure in Bondage in any one by the deceit, whisper thou not behind their back to others; but let the Witness in thee which sees the deceit, and suffers with the pure that is pressed down by it, let it declare and witness forth the mind of the living God against the deceit, and it will cut it down, and the pure holy Seed will be set at liberty, and thy conscience will be kept clean unto the Lord in discharging thy duty. And so will thy captivated Brother or Sister be restored again ... and then thou wilt have union together in that which is pure forever in the Lord.

And the eternal God of Power keep you all his dear children in his pure wisdom, to walk faithfully with him, and one with another, and the blessing of the Lord God almighty be with you all forever. (Dewsbury 23)

Acknowledgments

Many people have helped this project forward. First and foremost is Frances Taber, with her deep knowledge and insight about Quaker spirituality, and her long partnership with Bill Taber in life and service. As described in the preface, Fran encouraged me to take up the task, and she has read and discussed successive drafts over the years it has been in process. I am grateful for her discerning friendship.

I am indebted to Darcy Drayton, my life-partner, who (in addition to the patience and forbearance by which spouses support book writing) made important direct contributions to the book, reading carefully and insightfully what was actually on the page, while helping me figure out how it might be more useful, truthful, accessible, or graceful.

Particular thanks to Hugh Barbour, whose warm encouragement and close reading brought to bear his remarkable learning, his spiritual insight and passion, and his humor in a daunting, but inspiriting, commentary on an early draft of the book. Jerry Frost and Michael Birkel also read carefully and sympathetically, bringing both their scholarly knowledge and their appreciation for the value this material continues to offer to Friends and others.

Several other Friends and "reading elders" gave time, thought, and valuable comment on various drafts, and I am happy to thank Lynn Taber, Eric Edwards, and Cathy Whitmire. Ken and Katharine Jacobsen and Susan Smith encouraged me to offer a retreat at the Friends Center of Ohio Yearly Meeting, and that weekend was both challenging and instructive, as was a subsequent weekend at Pendle Hill—thanks to all who attended these weekends. I am aware of many others who have helped with encouragement, comments, and questions.

I am grateful that Eileen R. Kinch has been my editor. I needed a good editor, and she is one; but she is also a concerned and knowledgeable Friend, and I have valued her readings and learned from her suggestions and comments. Thanks to Tom Etherington for the index, and for encouragement and good conversation over many years. I am also grateful for Christine Greenland's work in managing the project for the Tract Association of Friends, and for her informed and concerned comments and care.

I am grateful to the Obadiah Brown Benevolent Fund and the Mosher Book and Tract Fund of New England Yearly Meeting, whose grants made the printing of the book possible, and whose expressions of support and interest were encouraging.

As with any book, the writer's community is an essential source of its virtues. The community enabling this book includes Bill Taber and the great cloud of witnesses whose words have been offered here. I, Brian, take responsibility for errors or insufficiencies, mindful of the great blessings that have come my way because of this opportunity.

Works Cited

Australia Yearly Meeting of the Religious Society of Friends. *This we can say: Australian Quaker life, faith and thought.* Kenmore, Queensland: Australia Yearly Meeting of the Religious Society of Friends, 2003.

Bacon, Margaret Hope, ed. *Wilt thou go on my errand? Three 18th century journals of Quaker women ministers.* Wallingford, PA: Pendle Hill Publications, 1994.

Barbour, Hugh. "Five tests for discerning a true leading." Philadelphia: Tract Association of Friends, n.d. http://www.tractassociation.org/tracts/tests-discerning-true-leading/

Barbour, Hugh. "The 'openings' of Fox and Bunyan." In *New Light on George Fox, 1624-1691.* Ed. M. Mullett. York: William Sessions Ltd, 1991. 129-143.

— . *The Quakers in Puritan England.* New Haven: Yale University Press, 1964.

— . "Christ and truth." *Quaker Religious Thought* IV, no. 1 (1962): 2-15.

Barclay, A. R., ed. *Letters, etc., of Early Friends.* Vol. 11. London, Darton & Harvey, 1847.

Barclay, Robert. *An apology for the true Christian divinity.* 1678. Reprint, Glenside, PA: Quaker Heritage Press, and Warminster, PA: Peter D. Sippel, 2002.

Beck, William and T. Frederick Ball. *The London Friends' Meetings.* London: F. Bowyer Kitto, 1869.

Benson, Lewis. "On being moved by the Spirit to minister in public worship." *New Foundation Publications* no. 4 (1979): 48-51.

Blackborrow, Sarah. *A Visit to the spirit in prison.* In Garman, M., J. Applegate, M Benefiel, and D. Meredith, eds., *Hidden in plain sight: Quaker women's writings 1650-1700.* Wallingford, PA: Pendle Hill Publications, 1996. 47-57.

Bownas, Samuel. *An account of the life, travels, and Christian experiences of Samuel Bownas, a minister of the Gospel in the Society of Friends.* In *Friends Library*, Vol. III. 1839. 1-70.

Braithwaite, J. B. *Memoirs of Joseph John Gurney* (in 2 volumes). Philadelphia: Lippincott, Grambo & Co., 1854.

Branson, Ann. *Journal of Ann Branson.* Philadelphia: Wm. H. Pile's Sons, Printers, 1892.

Brayshaw, A. N. *The Quakers: their story and message.* London: Friends Home Service Committee, 1969.

— . *The things that are before us: the Swarthmore Lecture for 1926.* London: The Swarthmore Press, Ltd., 1926.

Brinton, Howard H. *Friends for 300 years.* New York: Harper & Brothers Publishers, 1952.

— . "Friends for seventy-five years." *The Bulletin of the Friends Historical Association* 49, no.1 (1960): 3-20.

— . *Prophetic ministry.* Wallingford, PA: Pendle Hill, n.d. Pendle Hill Pamphlet 54.

Burnyeat, John. *The truth exalted in the writings of that eminent and faithful servant of Christ, John Burnyeat.* London: Thomas Northcott, 1691.

Coale, Benjamin. Memorial notice of Loveday Hambly. *The Friend,* Philadelphia. Vol. XVII, no. 21 (1844). 165-6.

Capper, Mary. *A memoir of Mary Capper, lately of Birmingham, a minister of the Society of Friends.* Philadelphia: Association of Friends for the dissemination of religious and useful knowledge, 1860.

Cock, Luke. "Sermon of the Weeping Cross." In *The Friend,* vol XV, no. 35 (1842), quoted in London Yearly Meeting of the Religious Society of Friends 1960, §42.

Conran, John. *A journal of the life and Gospel labours of John Conran.* Philadelphia: Henry Longstreth, 1877.

Crisp, Stephen. *The Christian experiences, Gospel labours and writings of that ancient servant of Christ, Stephen Crisp.* In *Friends' Library,* vol 14.1850. 134-278.

— . *Scripture Truth Demonstrated in a Series of Sermons or Declarations of Stephen Crisp.* Philadelphia: Joseph James, 1787.

Dandelion, Pink. *A sociological analysis of the theology of Quakers: The silent revolution.* Lampeter: Edwin Mellen Press, 1996.

Dewsbury, William. *The faithful testimony of that antient servant of the Lord, and minister of the everlasting gospel William Dewsbery; his books, epistles and writings, collected and printed for future service.* London: Andrew Sowle,1689.

Doncaster, Phoebe. *John Stephenson Rowntree: his life and work.* London: Headley Brothers, 1908.

Drayton, Brian. *James Nayler Speaking.* Wallingford, PA: Pendle Hill Publications, 2011. Pendle Hill Pamphlet 413.

— . *Unity, disunity, diversity OR Some mysteries of the Holy Spirit's LIFE at work in its body's members. A letter to New England Friends.* Boston: Beacon Hill Friends House, 2007.

— . *On living with a concern for Gospel ministry.* Philadelphia: Quaker Press, 2005.

Dymond, Joseph John. *Gospel Ministry in the Society of Friends: A series of letters.* London: Edward Hicks, Jun., 1892.

Emmott, E.B. *Loving service: A record of the life of Martha Braithwaite.* London: Headley Brothers, 1896.

Evans, Joshua. *A journal of the life, travels, religious exercises, and labours in the work of the ministry.* Philadelphia: John & Isaac Comly, 1837.

Fardelmann, C. L. *Nudged by the Spirit: Stories of people responding to the still, small voice of God.* Wallingford, PA: Pendle Hill Publications, 2001.

— . (1986) "Right use of time." *Friends Journal* 32, no. 4 (March 1, 1986): 8-9.

First Publishers of Truth. See Penney, N.

Fowler, Robert. *A True Relation Of The Voyage Undertaken By Me Robert Fowler, With My Small Vessel Called The " Woodhouse;" But Performed By The Lord, Like As He Did Noah's Ark, Wherein He Shut Up A Few Righteous Persons And Landed Them Safe, Even At The Hill Ararat.* 1657. In Bowden, James. *History of the Society of Friends in America.* London: Charles Gilpin, 1850. Vol. 1, 63-66.

Fox, George. *Journal.* See Nickalls, John L.

— . Epistles in *Works*, vol. 7 & 8.

— . *Works.* Vols 1-8. Philadelphia: M.T.C. Gould, 1831. New Foundation Fellowship, 1990.

Friends' Library. William Evans and Thomas Evans, eds. 14 vols. Philadelphia: Joseph Rakestraw for the editors, 1837-1850.

Graham, John W. *The Quaker ministry.* Swarthmore Lecture, 1925. London: The Swarthmore Press Ltd., 1925.

— . *Psychical experiences of Quaker ministers.* London: Friends Historical Society, 1933.

Gratton, John. *A journal of the life of that ancient servant of Christ, John Gratton.* In *Friends Library,* vol IX. 1845. 290-359.

Griffith, John. *Journal of John Griffith.* London: n.p., 1779.

Grubb, Sarah Lynes. *A brief account of the life and religious labors of Sarah Grubb.* Philadelphia: The Tract Association of Friends, 1863.

Grundy, Martha Paxson, ed. *Resistance and obedience to God: memoirs of David Ferris.* Philadelphia: Friends General Conference, 2001.

Harvey, T. Edmund. "Our Quaker ministry since the cessation of recording." *Friends Quarterly Examiner* 80 (1946): 187-192.

Hicks, Edward. *Memoirs of the life and religious labors of Edward Hicks. Written by himself.* Philadelphia: Merrihew & Thompson, Printers, 1851.

Hicks, Elias. *Journal.* New York: Isaac Hopper, 1832.

Hoag, Joseph. *Journal of the life of Joseph Hoag, an eminent minister of the Gospel in the Society of Friends.* Auburn, NY: Knapp and Peck, Printers, 1861.

Howgill, Francis. *The Dawnings of the Gospel Day, and its Light and Glory discovered, by a faithful and valiant follower of the Lamb, and labourer in the work and service of God, and a sufferer for the testimony of Jesus.* [London]: 1676.

— . "Testimony concerning the life, death, tryals, travels, and labours of Edward Burrough." In *The memorable works of a son of thunder and consolation.... Edward Burroughs.* London, 1672.

Hudson, Elizabeth. *The Journal of Elizabeth Hudson.* In Bacon, 121-274.

Janney, Samuel. *Memoirs of Samuel M. Janney: Late of Lincoln, Loudoun County, Va.*

A Minister in the Religious Society of Friends. Second ed. Philadelphia: Friends' Book Association, 1881.

Jenkins, James. *The Records and recollections of James Jenkins.* In *Texts and Studies in Religion*, Vol. 18, edited by J. William Frost. New York: The Edwin Mellen Press, 1984.

Jones, Rufus M. *An interpretation of Quakerism.* http://www.pym.org/publications/pym-pamphlets/an-interpretation-of-quakerism/ Accessed 10/12/14.

Kelly, Thomas. "The Gathered Meeting." In *The eternal promise*, ed. R.M. Kelly, 72-89. Richmond, IN: Friends United Press, 1977.

London Yearly Meeting of the Religious Society of Friends. *Christian Faith and Practice in the experience of the Religious Society of Friends.* London: London Yearly Meeting, 1960.

Merton, Thomas. *Conjectures of a guilty bystander.* Garden City, NY: Image Books. 1968.

Moore, Ann. *The Journal of Ann Moore.* In Bacon, 283-385.

Morris, Susanna. *The Journal of Susanna Morris.* In Bacon, 33-120.

Moulton, Phillips P. *The Journal and major essays of John Woolman.* New York: Oxford University Press, 1971.

Nayler, James. *The Works of James Nayler.* Vols 1-4. Glenside, PA: Quaker Heritage Press, 2003-2009.

Nickalls, John L., ed. *The Journal of George Fox.* Cambridge: at the University Press, 1952.

Nuttall, Geoffrey F. *To the refreshing of the Children of Light.* Wallingford, PA: Pendle Hill, 1959. Pendle Hill Pamphlet 101.

Penington, Isaac. *The works of Isaac Penington, a minister of the Gospel in the Society of Friends.* Vols. 1 to 4. Glenside, PA: Quaker Heritage Press, 1995-1997.

Penn, William. *The rise and progress of the people called Quakers.* Reprint edition. Richmond, IN: Friends United Press, 1980.

Pen pictures of London Yearly Meeting 1789-1833. First Part. London: Friends Historical Society, 1907.

Penney, Norman, ed. *The First Publishers of Truth.* London: Headley Brothers, 1907.

Ratcliff, Mildred. *Memoranda and correspondence of Mildred Ratcliff.* Philadelphia: Friends Bookstore, 1890.

Routh, Martha. Memoir of the life, travels, and religious experiences. York: W Alexander & Son, 1823.

Rutty, John. *A spiritual diary and soliloquies.* Second Edition. London: James Phillips. 1796.

Scott, Job. *The works of that eminent minister of the Gospel, Job Scott, late of Providence, Rhode Island.* 2 vols. Philadelphia: John Comly, 1831.

— . *Essays on Salvation by Christ and the debate which followed their publication.* Glenside, PA: Quaker Heritage Press, 1993.

Skidmore, Gil. *Strength in weakness: writings by eighteenth-century Quaker women.* Oxford: Rowman & Littlefield Publishers, Inc., 2003.

Stamper, Francis. "God has laid help upon one that is mighty." in Burns, P.J. and T. H.S. Wallace, eds. . *The concurrence and unanimity of the people called Quakers as evidenced by some of their sermons.* Camp Hill, PA: Foundation Publications, 2010. pp. 246-262

Stephenson, Sarah. *Memoirs of the life and travels in the service of the Gospel, of Sarah Stephenson.* In *Friends Library* vol IV. 1840. 171-214.

Taber, Frances I. *Finding the taproot of simplicity: a movement between inner knowledge and outer action.* Wallingford, PA: Pendle Hill Publications, 2009. Pendle Hill Pamphlet 400.

— . *Come aside and rest awhile.* Wallingford, PA: Pendle Hill Publications, 1997. Pendle Hill Pamphlet 335.

Taber, William P. "The theology of the inward imperative: travelling Quaker ministry of the middle period." *Quaker Religious Thought* 18, no. 4 (1980): 3-19.

— . *The Eye of Faith: A history of Ohio Yearly Meeting, Conservative.* Barnesville, OH: Ohio Yearly Meeting of Friends, 1985.

— . "Quaker ministry: the inward motion and the razor's edge." 1996. http://www.quaker.org/pendle-hill/taber.html. Accessed 7/20/04.

Thomas, A. L. *J. Bevan Braithwaite: A Friend of the XIX Century.* London: Hodder, 1919.

Whitehead, George, ed.. *A Collection of Sundry Books, Epistles and Papers written by James Nayler.* Cincinnati: B.C. Stanton, 1829. [reprint of 1716 London edition]

Whitman, Walt. "Notes (such as they are) founded on Elias Hicks." In *Prose Works.* Philadelphia: David McKay, 1892. Bartleby.com, 2000. http://www.bartleby.com/229/5021.html. Accessed 10/13/14.

Wilson, Lloyd Lee. *Essays on the Quaker vision of Gospel Order.* Wallingford, PA: Pendle Hill Publications, 1993.

Woolman, John. *Journal and major essays.* See Moulton, Phillips P.

— . *Journal of John Woolman*, ed. J.G. Whittier. London: Andrew Melrose, 1898.

— . *Worship.* Pendle Hill Pamphlet #51 Wallingford, PA: Pendle Hill Publications, 1950.

Index

Quotations are indicated in italics;
Chapter emphases are in bold

Index to Bible Quotations